Wal

# teach® yourself

typing

pitman publishing

revised by Bettina croft BA Dip RSA

for over 60 years, more than 40 million people have learnt over 750 subjects the **teach yourself** way, with impressive results.

be where you want to be with **teach yourself**

For UK orders: please contact Bookpoint Ltd, 130 Milton Park, Abingdon, Oxon OX14 4SB. Telephone: +44 (0)/1235 827720. Fax: +44 (0)/1235 400454. Lines are open 09.00–18.00, Monday to Saturday, with a 24-hour message answering service. Details about our titles and how to order are available at www.teachyourself.co.uk

For USA order enquiries: please contact McGraw-Hill Customer Services, PO Box 545, Blacklick, OH 43004-0545, USA. Telephone: 1-800-722-4726. Fax: 1-614-755-5645.

For Canada order enquiries: please contact McGraw-Hill Ryerson Ltd, 300 Water St, Whitby, Ontario L1N 9B6, Canada. Telephone: 905 430 5000. Fax: 905 430 5020.

Long renowned as the authoritative source for self-guided learning – with more than 40 million copies sold worldwide – the **teach yourself** series includes over 300 titles in the fields of languages, crafts, hobbies, business, computing and education.

*British Library Cataloguing in Publication Data*: a catalogue record for this title is available from The British Library.

*Library of Congress Catalog Card Number:* On file.

First published in UK 2003 by Hodder Headline Plc, 338 Euston Road, London, NW1 3BH.

First published in US 2003 by Contemporary Books, A Division of The McGraw-Hill Companies, 1 Prudential Plaza, 130 East Randolph Street, Chicago, Illinois 60601 USA.

The **teach yourself** name is a registered trade mark of Hodder Headline
Computer hardware and software brand names mentioned in this book are protected by their respective trademarks and are acknowledged.

Typeset by MacDesign, Southampton
Printed in Great Britain for Hodder Education, a division of Hodder Headline, 338 Euston Road, London NW1 3BH, by Cox & Wyman Ltd, Reading, Berkshire.

Hodder Headline's policy is to use papers that are natural, renewable and recyclable products and made from wood grown in sustainable forests. The logging and manufacturing processes are expected to conform to the environmental regulations of the country of origin.

Impression number    10 9 8 7 6 5 4 3
Year                 2007 2006 2005

# contents

iii

|  | preface | v |
|----|---------------------------------|-----|
| 01 | **getting started** | **1** |
|    | what do you need? | 2 |
|    | Word | 4 |
|    | entering and editing text | 6 |
|    | margins | 9 |
|    | paper size and orientation | 10 |
|    | saving | 12 |
|    | opening files | 13 |
|    | printing | 14 |
| 02 | **touch typing** | **16** |
|    | the touch method | 17 |
|    | the standard keyboard | 17 |
| 03 | **the guide key row** | **20** |
|    | the home keys | 21 |
| 04 | **the top alpha row** | **28** |
|    | the row above the guide keys | 29 |
| 05 | **the bottom row** | **35** |
|    | the remaining alpha keys | 36 |
| 06 | **the figure and symbol row** | **42** |
|    | the top row of the keyboard | 43 |
| 07 | **the shift keys and symbols** | **49** |
|    | shift keys | 50 |
|    | roman numerals | 58 |
|    | special characters and symbols | 59 |
| 08 | **speed development** | **62** |
|    | copying practice | 63 |
|    | copying exercises | 63 |

| | 09 | **punctuation** | **77** |
|---|---|---|---|
| | | punctuation marks | 78 |
| | | capitals | 83 |
| | | open and closed punctuation | 84 |
| | | punctuation summary | 85 |
| | 10 | **formatting documents** | **87** |
| | | presentation and layout | 88 |
| | | formatting text | 88 |
| | | paragraph formatting | 91 |
| | | templates | 97 |
| | | spell checking | 100 |
| | 11 | **business correspondence** | **102** |
| | | business letters | 103 |
| | | envelope addressing | 111 |
| | | memorandums | 114 |
| | | postcards | 115 |
| | | linked themes | 116 |
| | | meetings | 127 |
| | 12 | **deciphering manuscript** | **131** |
| | | working from handwritten copy | 132 |
| | | correction signs | 132 |
| | | the linked theme exercises | 134 |
| | 13 | **tabular work** | **149** |
| | | tabs | 150 |
| | | tables | 153 |
| | 14 | **speed tests** | **161** |
| | | repetition practice | 162 |
| | | strokes and words | 162 |
| | | speed test practice | 162 |
| | | calculation of errors | 163 |
| | 15 | **difficult spellings** | **173** |
| | 16 | **abbreviations** | **179** |
| | 17 | **key to the exercises** | **186** |
| | | **taking it further** | **199** |
| | | **index** | **201** |

# preface

Most people want to be able to type quickly and accurately, prepare their own correspondence, understand handwritten manuscript work and display a variety of business documents. If you study this book you will rapidly be able to attain these goals with ease.

This book has been specially designed for those who find it difficult to attend recognised training centres for regular tuition. The aim of attaining a good average speed of 40–50 words per minute has been allowed for by providing a section with speed tests which are simple to use and from which it is easy to work out your rate of progress. It is recommended that daily practice sessions are the ideal way of learning but, whatever time you can spend, the personal effort you put into practising is of vital importance.

This latest edition of *Teach Yourself Typing* has been updated and revised extensively so that you can quickly master keyboard operation on any type of computer which has a standard keyboard. Guidance is given on the best ways of learning to operate these keyboards, and to develop accuracy at speed. With this book you can quickly learn how to produce mailable letters, various types of frequently-used business documents, all your own personal correspondence, tabulated work and examples of other data now required in modern offices.

# 01 getting started

# What do you need?

If you want to learn to touch type, you need a suitable keyboard. This can be the keyboard of a personal computer – either a PC or an Apple – or a typewriter. All that is essential is that the keys are in the standard QWERTY arrangement.

Keyboards, in English-speaking countries, have used this layout since the early days of typewriters. Originally, keys were arranged in this way to *slow down* the typist – on manual typewriters if you type some sequences of characters too quickly, the arms that carry the letters can get tangled together! Nowadays the same layout is used because there are many millions of people who have learnt to touch type on a traditional keyboard, and this allows them to transfer their touch typing skills.

There are keyboards with more rational layouts, but they are not suitable. If you did learn to touch type on one of these, you could not use a normal keyboard.

Laptop computers are not recommended. Their keyboards are generally too small and the keys too closely packed together to allow the development of good typing habits.

In this book, it is assumed that you are using a computer, and that it will almost certainly be a Windows 98 or XP PC. If you are using an Apple computer, almost everything in the book will still apply, though some of the screenshots and some of the details of the procedures later in this chapter and in Chapter 10 will differ.

# Word processors

Any word processor can be used for learning touch typing and the key concepts and elements of document production.

All Windows PCs have **WordPad**, a simple but more than adequate word processor. Many now are supplied with **Word**, as part of a package of introductory software, and Word is the standard word processor in business and in education. It is also the most widely used word processor on Apple computers. This book assumes that you are using Word. The screenshots and details of the commands are from the Word 2000 version, but at this simple level of use, the earlier Word 98 and later XP versions are almost identical.

If you are using WordPad, you will likewise find very few differences, as WordPad is essentially a cut-down version of Word.

# Your work station

To carry out any keyboard work efficiently, a comfortable position will ensure better command during operation. For comfort, the workstation should have:

◆ Suitable desktop space

◆ An adjustable chair and sufficient desk room and leg room. The height of the chair in relation to the desktop should be adjusted so that the forearms are parallel to the desktop.

◆ A movable keyboard, with wrist support available. The wrist support is a padded cushion that allows the arms to rest with the hands just above the keyboard.

◆ A document holder at a suitable height, either at eye level or angled on the desktop.

◆ Adequate lighting, with blinds if necessary to minimise direct sunlight on the screen.

◆ Flicker-free, non-glare monitors, set at, or below, eye level.

◆ Adequate ventilation.

◆ Minimised printer noise (especially with impact printers).

# Word

The rest of this chapter is for those readers who have not used Word previously. It covers the basic concepts and techniques – enough to be able to use it to practise your keyboard skills, and a little more. If you already know how to enter and edit text, save files and print, then please skip ahead to Chapter 2.

Like most applications, Word can be started in several ways.

- Click the **Word** icon 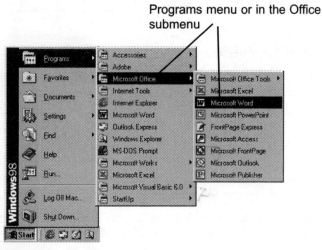 on the Desktop.
- Click the **Start** button, point to **Programs** and click **Microsoft Word** there or in the **Microsoft Office** submenu.

Click Microsoft Word in the Programs menu or in the Office submenu

**Figure 1.1** Starting Word from the Start menu.

## Why Word? Which Word?

Word is by far the most widely used word processor, especially in schools, colleges and in the home – places where we expect most of our readers to be. There are several versions of Word currently still in use, but at the simple level of this book, the differences in the commands and in the screen appearance are not significant.

## Word's tools

All of Word's commands and options can be reached through the menu system, but most can also be selected – more conveniently – through toolbar buttons. When Word first opens, two toolbars are displayed – the Standard and Formatting. All the tools that you need while using this book can be found on those toolbars, as shown in Figure 1.2.

◆ Start Word and find the tools labelled here. Point to each in turn and wait for the tooltip to appear. This will give its name and keyboard shortcut – if one is available.

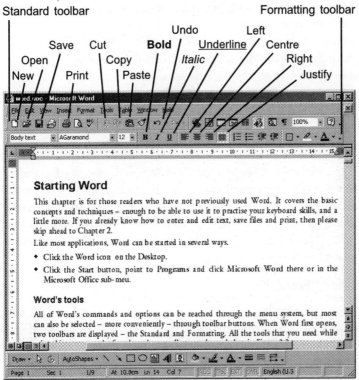

Standard toolbar — Formatting toolbar

New, Open, Save, Print, Cut, Copy, Paste, Bold, Italic, Undo, Underline, Left, Centre, Right, Justify

**Figure 1.2** The Microsoft Word screen, showing the main controls. Another ten toolbars are available and can be opened as needed, via the **View > Toolbars** menu.

# Entering and editing text

## Entering text

To create new text, type it in through the keyboard. The text will appear at the insertion point, which is marked by a flashing line. If the insertion point is not where you want it, move it into place with the arrow keys or point and click with the mouse.

### Wordwrap and new lines

When you reach the right-hand side of the working area *keep typing*! Word automatically starts a new line when needed, carrying the word down to the next line if it won't fit. This is known as **wordwrap**. If you later change the size of the text or the size of the margins, so that more or fewer words will fit on a line, Word will rewrap the text to suit the new settings.

Press [**Enter**] at the end of a paragraph, heading or bullet point to force the following text to start on a new line.

### Correcting errors

If you make a mistake and spot it immediately, use [**Backspace**] to rub out the character(s) that you have just typed. If you find a mistake later, click the insertion point into the text and use [**Backspace**] to rub out characters to its left, or [**Delete**] to erase to the right. You can also use either key to delete a selected block of text (see the next page for how to select text).

### Insert/Overwrite

If you start typing within some existing text, the new text will push the old text along to make room. This is *Insert* mode. If you want the new text to replace the old, press [**Insert**] to switch to *Overwrite* mode. Press [**Insert**] again to return to Insert mode.

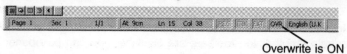

Overwrite is ON

**Figure 1.3**   The Insert/Overwrite mode indicator.

# Editing text

Word processing on computers has replaced the use of typewriters for one reason above all others – when you are word processing you can edit text far more efficiently. Mistakes are easily corrected and you can copy and move text without having to retype it.

## Selecting text

Before you can do any kind of editing on a block of text, you must first select it. A 'block' can be any size, from a single character to the whole document. How you select depends upon how big a block you want.

**To select with the mouse:**

| | |
|---|---|
| *a word* | double-click anywhere in the word |
| *a line* | click in the margin to the left of the line |
| *a paragraph* | triple-click anywhere in the paragraph |
| *any other text* | click at the start of the block and drag to the end. |

**To select with keys:**

| | |
|---|---|
| *all the text* | press [**Control**] and [**A**] |
| *any size block* | move the insertion point to the start of the block, hold down [**Shift**] and move to the end using… |
| *Arrows* | one character left or right, one line up or down |
| | one word left or right if [**Control**] is held down |
| *Home* | start of line; start of text with [**Control**] |
| *End* | end of line; end of text with [**Control**] |
| *PgUp* | one screenful up |
| *PgDn* | one screenful down |

### Cut, Copy and Paste

If you look at the Edit menu of any Windows application, you will find the commands **Cut**, **Copy** and **Paste**. You will also find them on the short menu that opens when you right-click on a selected object. These are used for copying and moving data within and between applications.

- **Copy** copies the selected block of text, picture, file or other object into a special part of memory called the *Clipboard*.

- **Cut** deletes the selected data from the original application, but places a copy into the Clipboard.

- **Paste** copies the data from the Clipboard into a different place in the same application, or into a different application – as long as this can handle data in that format.

The data normally remains in the Windows Clipboard until new data is copied or cut into it, or until Windows is shut down.

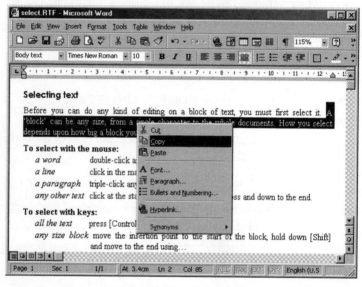

**Figure 1.4** The short menu offers the quickest route to the Cut and Paste commands. If the Clipboard is empty, Paste will be 'greyed out' or omitted from the menu.

## The Office Clipboard

A simple **Edit > Paste** pastes in the last item cut or copied, but since the 2000 version, Word has had its own Clipboard that can hold up to 12 or more items. If you open the Clipboard toolbar, you can select any single item to paste, or click **Paste All** to copy all the items at once.

# Margins

The margins are the areas around the edge of the page where text cannot be typed (except for headers and footers – see below). They are normally the same for the whole document.

The main margin settings determine the distances from the page edges. The defaults are 1 inch (2.54 cm) for the top and bottom, and 1.25 inches (3.17 cm) on the left and right.

The *gutter* is extra margin to allow for stapling or binding, and can be either on the left or top of the page.

Where pages are to be printed on both sides, and then bound, the left and right-hand pages may be different. If so, turn on *Mirror margins*, then set the inside and outside margins.

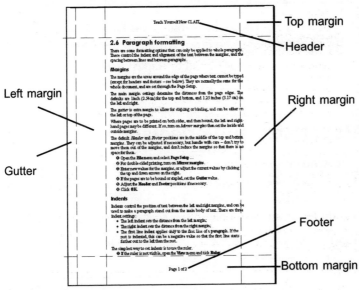

**Figure 1.5** Margins and page layout.

**To set the margins:**

1 Open the **File** menu and select **Page Setup…**

2 For double-sided printing, turn on **Mirror margins**.

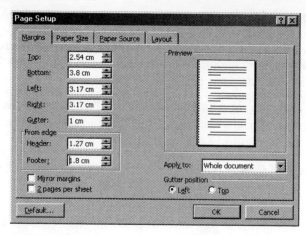

**Figure 1.6** The **Page Setup** dialog box, with the settings adjusted to give a small gutter on the left, and a deeper bottom margin.

3 Enter new values for the margins, or adjust the current values by clicking the up and down arrows on the right.

4 If the pages are to be bound or stapled, set the **Gutter** value.

5 Click **OK**.

# Paper size and orientation

The standard size of office paper in the UK is A4 (210 mm × 297 mm). The smaller A5 size (210 mm x 148 mm) is also used for very short letters and private correspondence. Your copy of Word should be set up for A4 paper, but check and correct if necessary.

Paper of any size can be printed in *portrait* or *landscape* orientation.

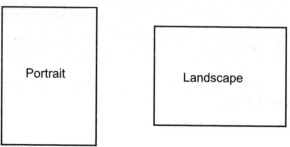

Portrait

Landscape

Almost all business letters, reports, memos and other material is printed portrait. The landscape orientation is typically used for printing spreadsheets, tables, charts or handouts, where the image is wider than it is high.

Whatever the orientation, paper is always put in the printer in the same way – for landscape printing, the image is rotated within the computer before being sent to the printer.

Set the paper size and orientation on the **Paper Size** tab of the **Page Setup** dialog box.

**To set the paper size or orientation:**

1  Open the **File** menu and select **Page Setup...**

2  Click on the **Paper Size** tab to bring its panel to the front.

3  Click the arrow to the right of the **Paper Size** slot and select the size from the list that drops down.

4  Click on the word or the radio button to the left to select *Portrait* or *Landscape* in the **Orientation** area.

5  Click **OK** to close the dialog box.

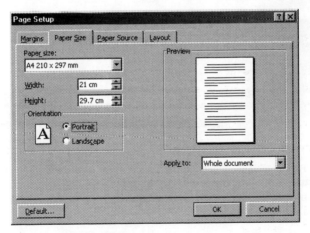

**Figure 1.7** The **Paper Size** tab, set up for standard A4 paper in portrait orientation.

# Saving

Documents should be saved regularly. If you do not save your work, it will be lost if the PC is turned off or the system crashes.

The first time that you save the file, you need to give it a name and decide on the folder in which it will be stored. When you save it again, you will normally simply replace the existing file with a new copy – and this can be done with a single click of a button. You can also save the file with a new name or in a different folder, retaining the old version as a backup or for future reference.

1 Open the **File** menu and select **Save As...** the **Save As** dialog box will appear.

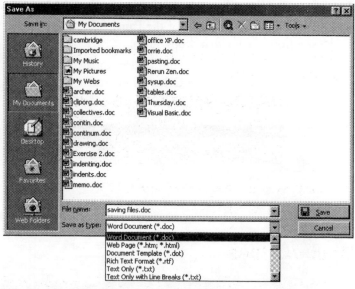

**Figure 1.8** The **Save As** dialog box. Use this when saving a document for the first time, or when resaving it with a new name or in a different place.

2 Select the folder in which to save the file. Open the **Save in** list and select the drive, then work down to the folder as necessary.

3 A filename will be suggested, based on the first words in the document. Edit or replace it to give a name you will remember.

4   The **Save as type** is normally *Word Document*, but a file can be saved as a *Web page*, or as *Text* or in other formats.

5   Click **Save**.

**To resave the file with the same name:**

♦   Click 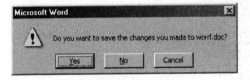 the **Save** button – that's it!

**To resave the file with a new name or in a different folder/drive:**

♦   Open the **File** menu and select **Save As...** then complete the dialog box as required.

## Closing files

When you have finished work on a file, it should be closed. If you have not saved the latest version, you will be prompted to do so.

1   Open the **File** menu and select **Close**.

2   If the file has been changed since the last save, you will be prompted to save it.

Click **Yes** to save, **No** to close without saving or **Cancel** to return to the open document.

# Opening files

When you want to read or work on a file again, it must be opened before you can work on it again.

**To open a file:**

1   Open the **File** menu and select **Open**.

2   At the **Open** dialog box, work your way through to the folder in which the file is stored.

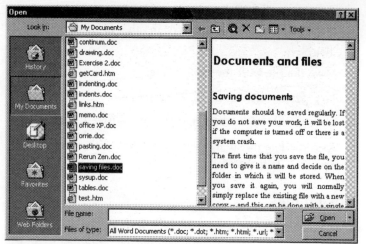

**Figure 1.9** The **Open** dialog box.

3   If you cannot remember where the file is stored, but can remember when you last worked on it, click the **History** button and list the files in date order.

4   Click on a file to select it. If you are not sure that it is the right file, wait a moment and check it in the preview pane.

5   Click **Open**.

# Printing

**To print the document with the default settings** – which will usually mean printing one copy of all the pages, at normal quality on the printer connected to (or on a network, assigned to) your PC – simply click 🖨 the **Print** button on the Standard toolbar.

**To check or change the settings before printing:**

1   Open the **File** menu and select **Print...**

2   If you want to change the **Printer**, select one from the list.

3   Set the **Print Range**. This can be *All* pages, the *Current Page*, the *Selection* only, or identified *Pages*, e.g. 1,4,7 or 2-5,8.

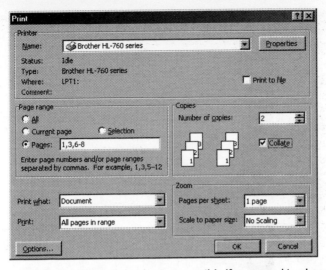

**Figure 1.10** The **Print** dialog box – open this if you need to change any of the settings before printing.

4   Set the **Number of copies**. If **Collate** is on, all the pages for the first copy will be printed before starting the next.

5   Click **OK** to print.

# 02

## touch typing

# The touch method

Today it is necessary first to learn touch typing in order to be a fast, accurate keyboard operator and to use the computers and other keyboard controlled machines found in modern offices.

This method has played an important part in typewriting progress since it is based on scientific principles. Typing by touch means that it is not necessary to glance from copy down to keyboard and back to what has been typed. The proficient typist locates the correct keys by touch and not by sight, and that is why blind people can become such excellent typists. Once learnt the movement becomes an automatic (subconscious) operation.

Each finger operates by relating only to the keys specifically allotted to it. Any confusion and strain are avoided as the fingers become, with practice, properly trained to respond instantly to the correct mental impulses and a reflex action occurs similar to the automatic effect of changing gears when driving a car. Eventually each finger moves in correct order to produce effortlessly a perfectly typed word.

# The standard keyboard

The standard method of fingering is used throughout this book. It is a logical fingering system and is easily learnt. The layout is known as the 'Qwerty keyboard' because of the word created by the first six letters of the top alphabetic row. The letters and main punctuation symbols are divided into three rows in this order:

Q W E R T Y U I O P

A S D F G H J K L ;

Z X C V B N M , .

In addition to these alphabet keys there are other keys for figures, commercial and other signs, and punctuation marks. Some of these do vary in position from one model to another.

As illustrated in Figure 2.1 opposite, the keyboard is divided into two approximately equal sections – one for each hand, and each finger is allotted a series of keys. The right thumb is used for the space bar.

Notice that only the main block of keys is shown as these are the only ones that are relevant for touch typing. The other sets – the function keys along the top, the cursor control keys to the right of the main block and the number pad on the far right – are used for special purposes and can only be reached by moving the hands.

## Keyboard diagrams

A diagram of the complete keyboard is essential for self-tuition, as it will help in memorising the keys during the early stages of learning. In each of the following practice exercises and on the facing page there is a diagram showing the division of the typewriter keyboard, with a clear indication of the sections allotted to the fingers of each hand. It is necessary to refer to this frequently during the keyboard learning period in order to memorise the location of the keys.

Left hand

Right hand

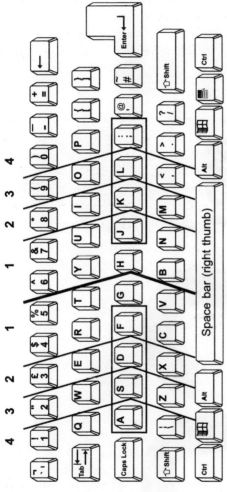

**Figure 2.1** Division of the keyboard for touch typing.

# 03

## the guide key row

# The home keys

The most important section of the typewriter keyboard will naturally receive first consideration. It consists of eight keys in the second row from the space bar, known as the 'home keys', and from these keys the sense of location of all the other keys will be developed.

These home keys are [A] [S] [D] [F] for the fingers of the left hand and [ ; ] [L] [K] [J] for the fingers of the right hand. They are often referred to as the 'guide keys', although it is generally considered that the guide keys are the two home keys operated by the little fingers – [A] and [ ; ].

The following diagram shows the arrangement of the home keys (the boxed-in sections):

During keyboard operation the tips of the fingers indicated in the diagram should rest lightly (so lightly that they do not actually depress the keys) on the home keys. The little finger of the left hand operates [A], and the third, second and first fingers operate the remaining keys for the left section – [S] [D] [F]. The little finger of the right hand operates the semicolon [ ; ], and the third, second and first fingers operate the remaining keys for the right section – [L] [K] [J].

Repeat aloud several times **A S D F** and **; L K J**, in this order, and during the repetition tap the respective fingers on the desk at equal intervals of time – one tap a second. This will give a clear picture of what is required.

## Key markers

On some keyboards, **[F]** and **[J]** have raised markers so that your index fingers can locate their home keys by touch.

## Keyboard practice

Start a new document in Word. Check that these settings are in use – and change them if necessary. **Style**: Normal; **Font**: Times New Roman; **Font size**: 10; **Align**: Left.

Place your fingers on the home keys, as shown in Figure 2.1 (page 19). If you remove your hands from the keyboard return your fingers to their home keys *without looking at the keyboard*.

Each key should be struck lightly and at equal intervals of time – one stroke a second until repeated practice makes an increase to two strokes a second possible. Getting a good, even rhythm is very important and the only way to achieve that is to start with a slow but regular beat. It is essential at this stage that there should be absolute accuracy and even depression of the keys; speed will come with regular practice.

Place the copy by the side of the keyboard. Make sure that it is in such a position that you can read the exercises easily without having to alter your position at the machine.

The four keys memorised for the left hand ([A] [S] [D] [F]) are required for the first line of Exercise 1 (on page 24), and, with the eyes on the copy, this combination of letters is to be repeated twelve times. While the home keys for the left hand are being struck for the first line, the fingers of the right hand should be resting lightly on their respective keys. The line numbers are inserted for reference only, and the reminders given with the exercises should be carefully noted before starting to type.

When the end of each line is reached, stretch the little finger on the right hand across and press the [**Enter**] key.

Now note the second line. This deals with the four keys memorised for the right hand ([;] [L] [K] [J]) and completes the eight home keys. The fingers of the left hand should be in the normal home keys position during the typing of the second line.

In the third and fourth lines the additional keys ([G] and [H]) are introduced; they are shown in the diagram at the head of the exercises. The first finger of the left hand will move slightly to the right from [F] to [G], and the first finger of the right hand will move slightly to the left from [J] to [H]. The other fingers should not be moved when the additional key is struck. Immediately after the depression of [G] or [H] the finger should return to its home key. Each series of letters in these lines finishes on the home keys for the first fingers – [F] and [J].

For the fifth and sixth lines the order has been varied. Repeated practice will ensure that, as each letter is read, the appropriate finger will respond to the direction by the brain and depress the key for the letter shown in the copy.

A space is required after each series of letters in the fifth and sixth lines, and the space bar should always be struck with the right-hand thumb, but the fingers should not leave their home key positions. The time taken for the depression of the space bar should be equal to that for a letter or character key; in this way correct rhythm will be maintained.

Each line in the exercises should be treated as a separate item and copied three times. After the repeated practice on each line, type at least one accurate copy of the whole exercise.

More work with the space bar is given in Exercise 2, and Exercises 3 and 4 consist of words built up from the home keys and the additional keys for the first finger of each hand.

After finishing each exercise examine the work and make a note of any mistakes. Try to find out the cause of any errors – uneven key depression, wrong fingers, etc. – and then type the corrections several times. If any of the typed letters are repeated when they should not be, it can be assumed that the keys are being pressed heavily, instead of being tapped with a staccato movement.

Finally, remember that this first stage of keyboard mastery is of special importance; it is with this second row of keys that the remainder of the keyboard is associated, and extended practice on the exercises will be well worth the time spent in this way.

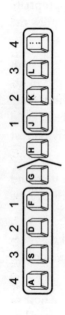

4 3 2 1    1 2 3 4

A S D F G H J K L ....

## Exercise 1

1. asdfasdfasdfasdfasdfasdfasdfasdfasdf

2. ;lkj;lkj;lkj;lkj;lkj;lkj;lkj;lkj;lkj

3. asdfgfasdfgfasdfgfasdfgfasdfgfasdfgf

4. ;lkjhj;lkjhj;lkjhj;lkjhj;lkjhj;lkjhj

5. fdsa jkl; fdsa jkl; fdsa dfas kj;l dfas

6. sfad lj;k sfad lj;k sfad sadf l;kj sadf

7. dad; sad; lad; lass; falls; fads; gag; flag; has;

8. a lass falls; dad has flags; a sad lad has a fad;

9. glass; gala; saga; flask; salad; jag; lash; gash;

10. a lad had a gag; a glass flask; dad adds a salad;

## Exercise 2

1. as ad af ag ;l ;k ;j ;h as ad af ag ;l ;k ;j ;h

2. ;l ;k ;j ;h as ad af ag ;l ;k ;j ;h as ad af ag

3. as ;l ad ;k af ;j ag ;h as ;l ad ;k af ;j ag ;h

4. sa l; da k; fa j; ga h; sa l; da k; fa j; ga h;

5. sd df sd df lk kj lk kj sd df sd df lk kj lk kj

6. gf fg gf fg jh hj jh hj gf fg gf fg jh hj jh hj

7. hall; halls; flash; shall; hag; gas; sags; daffs;

8. gala flags; a sad saga; a glass hall; daffs fall;

9. sash; dash; slash; hash; ask; galas; sagas; gags;

10. jags dash; sad sagas; dad asks a gag; glass sash;

**Reminders**: adopt correct position at keyboard; do not look at keyboard; fingers to rest lightly on home keys; right-hand thumb for space bar; equal intervals between each key depression; one stroke a second; the line numbers are for reference only. Type each line three times.

03 the guide key row

25

A S D F G H J K L ;
4 3 2 1 ... 1 2 3 4

## Exercise 3

1. sad; lag; sad; lag; sad; lag; sad; lag;

2. jag; has; jag; has; jag; has; jag; has;

3. fad; ask; fad; ask; fad; ask; fad; ask;

4. lad; aha; lad; aha; lad; aha; lad; aha;

5. gas; ash; gas; ash; gas; ash; gas; ash;

6. had; sag; had; sag; had; sag; had; sag;

7. dad has had a flag; ask a gag; has a flask glass;

8. flask; flasks; gala; galas; fad; fads; gas; lash;

9. add a gag; lads had fads; ash falls; ,glass flask;

10. gala salads; all flags fall; a lass adds a glass;

## Exercise 4

1. dash; half; dash; half; dash; half; dash; half;

2. lass; glad; lass; glad; lass; glad; lass; glad;

3. gall; hags; gall; hags; gall; hags; gall; hags;

4. flask shall flask shall flask shall flask shall

5. salad glass salad glass salad glass salad glass

6. galas flags galas flags galas flags galas flags

7. half a flag; glass hall; glad gag; flasks fall;

8. hags; sall; lags; dall; fall; slag; sags; lass;

9. dads ask; gas adds; a lass falls; half a salad;

10. all had salad; shall a lad dash; dad has a jag;

**Reminders**: right-hand thumb for space bar; first finger returns to home key after striking additional key; little movement of the wrists. Keep an even rhythm. Type each line three times.

# 04

## the top alpha row

# The row above the guide keys

The top row of the alpha keyboard includes ten additional letters of the alphabet, five for the fingers of each hand. The order in which they appear is shown in the following diagram:

As you have practised the guide keys in the previous chapter you should now find it possible to reach up from these keys to the row immediately above and this is the row from which the design of the keyboard gets its name – 'Qwerty'.

Each finger has to reach up to cover an additional key, [A] to [Q], [S] to [W], [D] to [E], and so on, with the exception of the fore-finger of each hand which, being stronger, covers two keys on the row above. The left forefinger moves from [F] to [T] and [F] to [R], and the right from [J] to [Y] and [J] to [U]. The remaining keys follow logically: [K] to [I], [L] to [O], [ ; ] to [P].

*Remember to keep your fingers hovering over the guide keys and reach up to strike the correct key. Do not lift the whole hand up one row.*

## The exercises

The following exercises contain some fingering drills incorporated into the keyboard training which will enable you to 'feel' your way up the keyboard to locate the required key, for example:

```
aqa sws ded frf
juj kik lol ;p;
ftf jyj ftf jyj
```

These are swiftly followed by words containing the new row of letters so that meaningful practice can take place using your new ability to type the extra vowels, i and e.

Q W E R T Y U I O P
A S D F G H J K L ....

4 3 2 1 1 2 3 4

## Exercise 5

1. aqa ;p; aqa ;p; aqa ;p; aqa ;p; aqa ;p;
2. sws lol sws lol sws lol sws lol sws lol
3. ded kik ded kik ded kik ded kik ded kik
4. frf juj frf juj frf juj frf juj frf juj
5. ftf jyj ftf jyj ftf jyj ftf jyj ftf jyj
6. gtg hyh gtg hyh gtg hyh gtg hyh gtg hyh
7. see sea lee lea tee tea the she fee gee gea
8. jeer fear leaf hear gear dear deer here peer rear
9. he fears the sea; she sees a dear rear; tea leaf;
10. she sees the red dear is here; they all hear her;

## Exercise 6

1. aqw ;po aqw ;po aqw ;po aqw ;po aqw ;po
2. swe loi swe loi swe loi swe loi swe loi
3. der kiu der kiu der kiu der kiu der kiu
4. frt juy frt juy frt juy frt juy frt juy
5. gtr hyu gtr hyu gtr hyu gtr hyu gtr hyu
6. qaw p;o wse oli edr iku qaw p;o wse oli edr iku
7. are is that was its at to this were few get you
8. pot spot quote equity query pro pride pear poorer;
9. it was quoted; there were a few; he spots a query;
10. was that a spot; that was poor; his pride appears;

**Reminders**: find home keys position without looking at the keyboard; the touch should be as light as possible; time for depression of space bar the same as for character key; examine work, encircle all errors and type corrections several times.

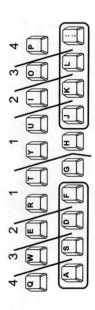

## Exercise 7

1. lap fit hay pay dog key for hye fur jay foes figs

2. deaf poll free pill gear oily tear holy read hill

3. hoop star hull lead loop dare steep gate pull fry

4. she feared steep hills; they pulled the dogs free

5. flay dial work goal fury girl dual dish fowl quay

6. spelt prowls shapes lapel shale palsy queue furls

7. ladder dapper figure shallow ferret dagger gossip

8. keep deaf ears to all gossip; the sea was shallow

9. fit the seat tightly; pull the dagger out please;

10. two star ships are early; today there are queues;

## Exercise 8: Consolidation

All these sentences are based on letters and/or words already practised in Exercises 1– 7 inclusive.

1. they are sure that they were right at that period

2. at their request the first few words were deleted

3. there is a good supply of hot water at this hotel

4. goods like those are sure to get you the top rate

5. he helped us to pass the press proofs of the list

6. the guard said that the lads had paid their fares

7. what was it that he saw at their park gates today

8. are there ladders outside the new houses for sale

9. he feared to tell her that they saw a yellow star

10. the queues were to the right of the theatre doors

**Reminders:** the hand not typing should remain in home keys position; examine work for accuracy.

Practise:

```
see lee fees deed

die lies fie kids
```

You will see that the forefingers of each hand have four times as much work to do since not only do they also cover [G] and [H] on the guide key row, but are used to reach up and across for [R] and [U], and finally across and upwards for [T] and [Y].

Practise:

```
fit feet fate jay hat hit yes yet
```

Your fingers will now be working in harmony to cover the whole of these two rows of the keyboard. You will also rapidly progress to the shift keys so that individual words with capital letters can be typed.

# 05

## the bottom row

# The remaining alpha keys

Having successfully mastered the guide key row and the row above, you can now progress to the remaining alphabetic keys on the bottom row. Study this diagram carefully.

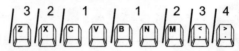

The movement of your fingers downwards and slightly to the left is necessary for the bottom row of keys. The fourth finger (or little finger) on the left hand has nothing to do at this stage, but it will be put to work later when we start to use the shift key on that side (see Chapter 7).

The following finger reaches require considerable perseverance in practising. Make sure that you first locate your fingers over the guide keys and then reach down to type with the third finger of the left hand:

szs szs szs szs szs szs szs

Do not allow the whole hand to move down the keyboard.

Using the third finger of the right hand reach down from [L] and type the comma.

l,l,l,l,l,l,l,l,l,l,l,l,l

Then using the fourth finger (little finger) of the right hand reach down from the semicolon to the full stop. (This finger will also cover the right-hand shift key in Chapter 7.)

;.;.;.;.;.;.;.;.;.;.;.;.;

Continue to practise the following reaches downwards first with the middle finger of the left hand and then with middle finger of the right until you can build up speed.

dxd dxd dxd dxd dxd dxd dxd

kmk kmk kmk kmk kmk kmk kmk

Finally, when you have practised all the fingering drills above to develop speed, progress to the reaches downwards from [F] to [C] with the left forefinger and then from [J] to [N] with the right forefinger:

```
fcf fcf fcf fcf jnj jnj jnj jnj
fcf fcf fcf fcf jnj jnj jnj jnj
```

You will notice again that the forefingers are doubling up on their workloads as they have also to cover the reaches across to [V] and [B] respectively (you will find stretching across to [B] needs practice):

```
fvf fvf fvf fvf fvf fvf fvf fvf
jbj jbj jbj jbj jbj jbj jbj jbj jbj
```

## The exercises

For the exercises in this chapter, keep hands hovering over the guide key rows and reach down to the keys. Practise each word for at least two lines before starting the sentences, and practise each fingering drill several times.

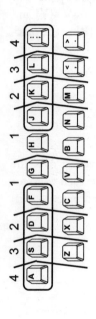

## Exercise 9

1. szs l,l szs l,l szs l,l ;.; ;.; ;.; ;.; ;.;

2. dxd kmk dxd kmk dxd kmk fcf jnj fcf jnj fcf jnj

3. fvf jbj fvf jbj fvf jbj fvf jbj fvf jbj

4. zxz ,m, cvc nbn zxz ,m, cvc nbn zxz ,m, cvc nbn

5. zoo man ebb car oxo mop van mad axe box ace coz

6. many boxes of mops can go to the zoo in the car

7. cat but cut not cot vet bet men eve ivy cry nib

8. a quiet time means less work for the van driver

9. zones mends above caters vendors bending oxygen

10. see how delicate the ozone layer is above earth

## Exercise 10

1. asz ;l, asz ;l, asz ;l, sdx lkm sdx lkm sdx lkm

2. dfc kjn dfc kjn dfc kjn fgv jhb fgv jhb fgv jhb

3. green fields and trees enable us to breathe air

4. aqa ;p. swz lo, dex kim frc jun gtv hyb aqa ;p.

5. p.p ,o, ex mim nib mid ice buzz nor inn own vie

6. ever nun viva bye buy ivy cot bat lobs mug tops

7. our batsmen played two very exciting games today.

8. time zone over lick oboe mean have care come zeal

9. cats have much more zeal in chasing mice than men

10. the new world time zones do vary by several hours

**Reminders**: set your own margin stops; eyes on copy; note downward movement from second row; full depression of shift key in the same time as that taken for character key.

## Exercise 11

1. cab ham van bad nag jam dab ban sax cad jab fan

2. and can mad lax bag jag bat nab ham act dam man

3. amend label flame naval panel glebe brake snake

4. vi.sor brick clays urban vodka codes lapel horse

5. chair mango docks neigh widow shame broth slant

6. sings penal chant handy spent chaos bench cycle

7. the cab came and the van went; mend the dam now

8. money well spent; labels are handy; red flames;

9. horses neigh; penalty codes are amended yearly;

10. extra time must be spent on exercises and diet;

## Exercise 12

1. face limb raze boil axe, the man can act and sing
2. cave bulk fact lion fax, ban jam and eat more veg
3. gave join care tame arc, can lions live in caves;
4. vast act ban wave exit, boil the bulk of the ham;
5. milk plum pun act over, the docks had vast waves;
6. hymn bin vase ice daze, urban areas have no cabs;
7. bulk oil is often used for new cars in the garage
8. save birthday cards for various charities to use.
9. plum and apple trees need careful pruning yearly.
10. the calcium contained in milk is very beneficial.

**Reminders**: cultivate a light and even touch, with a good rhythm; do not look at the keyboard
– eyes on the copy; examine typewritten work, encircle errors and type correct words.

05 the bottom row

05 the bottom row

# 06

## the figure and symbol row

# The top row of the keyboard

You can now type 26 letters of the alphabet, and punctuation marks for the semicolon, comma and full stop.

This chapter includes the row at the top of the main keyboard, which carries the Arabic numbers (1 to 0), the hyphen and the equals sign. From the diagram you can see that other signs are also on the upper portion of each figure key. These are obtained by using the shift keys in conjunction with the figure keys, as you will see in the next chapter.

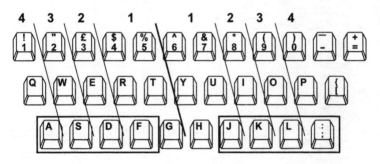

The forefingers of each hand will again double their workload as 4 and 5 have to be operated with left forefinger and 6 and 7 with the right forefinger. The reach from the guide key row is further than you have experienced so far and is slightly to the left of the corresponding keys in the top alpha row.

Again remember to keep the fingers hovering above the guide keys. Strike the relevant guide key, then the key from the row above and then reach up to the figure.

```
aql sw2 de3 fr4 gt5
hy6 ju7 ki8 lo9 ;p0
```

As you can see, the little finger of the right hand also reaches up and across to the right for the hyphen thus:

```
;p- ;p- p;- p;- ;p- p;-
```

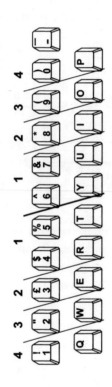

## Exercise 13

1. aq1 ;p0 aq1 ;p0 aq1 ;p0 sw2 1o9 sw2 1o9 sw2 1o9

2. de3 ki8 de3 ki8 de3 ki8 fr4 ju7 fr4 ju7 fr4 ju7

3. gt5 hy6 gt5 hy6 gt5 hy6 aq1 ;p0 sw2 1o9 de3 ki8

4. you have 27 benches and 93 chairs in stock now;

5. it will be 17 May today, and tomorrow is 18 May

6. computers can now store 750,000 new addresses

7. margins of 28 and 86 are used for text no 36780

8. he came – he saw – and then he conquered us all

9. shopping list – tea, bacon, 12 eggs, 1 kilo sugar

## Exercise 14

1. a1a ;o; a1a ;o; a1a ;o; s2s 191 s2s 191 s2s 191

2. d3d k8k d3d k8k d3d k8k f4f j7j f4f j7j f4f j7j

3. g5g h6h g5g h6h g5g h6h 132 425 262 728 293 038

4. numbers- 145 8979, 041-678 59403, 051-270 9634

5. the conjuror used 149 boxes – 16 tricks in each

6. please post leaflets to flats 39, 41, 45 and 63

7. he telephoned the new 661, 667, and 678 series.

8. 423,891 people will now be coming from 56 areas

**Reminder**: do not confuse the number 0 with the letter o; type each line three times
then type the whole exercise straight through at least twice

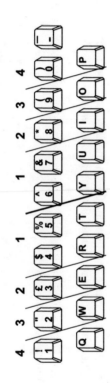

4  3  2  1  1  2  3  4

## Exercise 15

1. top 123 pip 345 try 678 our 132 pie 354 now 687

2. 213 rye 435 wet 768 toe 231 raw 453 pop 786 eye

3. pop try the top row – our 78 red cups were gone

4. put 3770 and 3120 out – the toy pup was too wet

5. all the 79 men cut the 40 yew trees and 56 oaks

6. quotes are very low for orders of 3,000 or more

## Exercise 16

1. tree 1234 weep 3456 peer 5678 quip 7890 prop 4321

2. rope 2342 wept 4563 pert 6785 part 9780 tour 2341

3. write your name on the list for tour number 46593

4. now order 360 spare tyres for your 19 office cars

5. look at part 7 and type out the 8th on micro card

6. pier 59 needs rope from the bulk naval store room

7. & is called an ampersand, and @ is the 'at' sign.

8. / is named 'slash' and is used for references etc

9. ' is single quotation mark or used for apostrophe

10. an asterisk is *, and " is used for double quotes

**Reminders:** keep eyes on copy during keyboard operation; make a note of all your errors and type corrections several times.

An even greater stretch is needed to reach the = sign, but this is highly unlikely to be used when typing text.

## The exercises

In the exercises in this chapter, the top row exercises have been incorporated with practice provided to cover the whole keyboard, including numbers.

Chapter 7 deals with the symbols produced using the [**Shift**] key with the keys in this row.

# 07

## the shift keys and symbols

# Shift keys

Each of the 48 keys on the main keyboard produces at least two characters. These may include a lower-case and capital (or upper-case) alphabetical character, a figure, symbol or punctuation mark. The keyboard diagram on page 51 shows all the miscellaneous characters and signs on the top portion of the keys. However, keyboards do vary a little, depending upon their age and whether they are on UK or US settings. Look in particular for the currency signs £, $, € the @ sign and the " double quotes. Do find out where they are on your own particular machine.

The [Shift] keys are used for the capital letters and characters shown on the top of the figure and symbol keys. There is a [Shift] on each side of the keyboard, at each end of the bottom row of keys. The [Shift] keys are operated by the little fingers of the opposite hands. If the character required is on the right-hand side of the keyboard, the left [Shift] must be depressed, and vice versa.

The use of the [Shift] key is different from that for the ordinary key stroke, as [Shift] must be held down during the striking of the character key on the opposite side of the keyboard. The timing of this depression should be the same as for a character key – and ensure that there is no break in the rhythm. The finger should return to its normal home key position immediately [Shift] is released.

## Caps Lock

The [Caps Lock] key should be used when several capital letters are to be typed in succession. Press it once to turn it on. The Caps Lock indicator light on the top right of keyboard will glow. Do not forget to press [Caps Lock] to turn it off, after the capitals have been typed. The Caps Lock only affects the letter keys. You must hold down [Shift] to get the upper symbols on the figure and symbol keys.

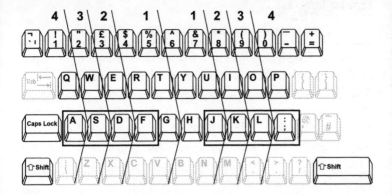

The first practice for [**Shift**] key operation will deal with associated keys of the second, third and fourth rows. The capitals (use [**Shift**]) are given for the second row, the lower-case letters for the third row and the miscellaneous characters (using [**Shift**]) for the fourth row. On some machines, the keys may differ from those shown for the top row. The appropriate alterations should therefore be made.

Depress the right-hand [**Shift**] to its full extent and use the little finger of the left hand to type A; release [**Shift**] and then type the lower-case letter in the third row for the same finger q, and again depress the right-hand shift key to type the exclamation mark(!) in the top row. Repeat these movements several times, as:

```
Aq! Aq! Aq! Aq! Aq! Aq! Aq! Aq!
```

Now combine the remaining keys for the left hand in the three rows under construction, as:

```
Sw" Sw" Sw" Sw" Sw" Sw" Sw" Sw"
Def Def Def Def Def Def Def Def
Fr$ Fr$ Fr$ Fr$ Fr$ Fr$ Fr$ Fr$
Gt% Gt% Gt% Gt% Gt% Gt% Gt% Gt%
```

Similar movements by the right hand and the depression of the left [**Shift**] will complete the remaining six upper-case characters of the top row.

Type six lines, as:

```
:p)  :p)  :p)  :p)  :p)  :p)  :p)  :p)
:p_  :p_  :p_  :p_  :p_  :p_  :p_  :p_
Lo(  Lo(  Lo(  Lo(  Lo(  Lo(  Lo(  Lo(
Ki*  Ki*  Ki*  Ki*  Ki*  Ki*  Ki*  Ki*
Ju&  Ju&  Ju&  Ju&  Ju&  Ju&  Ju&  Ju&
Hy^  Hy^  Hy^  Hy^  Hy^  Hy^  Hy^  Hy^
```

The key at the extreme left of the top row produces the characters ` and ¬ with [**Shift**] held down. As neither have any use in normal text, there is little point in learning to touch type these.

## The remaining symbols

There are a set of symbols on the right of the keyboard that are operated mainly by the fourth finger of the right hand.

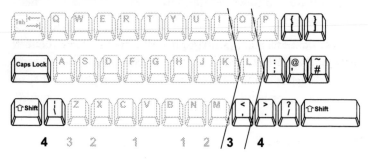

On the top alphabetic row are the square brackets [ and ]. When [**Shift**] is held down, these keys give the curly brackets { and }.

Stretch the little finger to type the square brackets, then hold down [**Shift**] and type the curly brackets. Practise:

```
;[;]  ;{;}  ;[;]  ;{;}  ;[;]  ;{;}
```

On the guide key row, the fourth finger's home key [ ; ] produces a colon with [**Shift**] held down. The finger must then extend to the right to get the apostrophe (') or the @ sign with [**Shift**], then further to the right to get the hash # or the tilde ~ with [**Shift**].

Practise: for the first set, type the three keys with [**Shift**] held down to give :@~ then without to produce ;'#. In the second set [**Shift**] is alternately pressed and released.

```
:@~  :@~  ;'#  ;'#  :@~  :@~  ;'#  ;'#

;@#  :'~  ;@#  :'~  ;@#  :'~  ;@#  :'~
```

On the bottom alpha row, use the third finger with [**Shift**] on the comma key to type the less than < sign. Use the fourth finger with [**Shift**] on the full stop key to type the greater than > sign. Stretch the little finger down and to the right to reach the forward slash / and the question mark ? with [**Shift**].

Hold down the left [**Shift**], and with the third right finger strike the key for the bottom row (the comma); with the little finger strike the key to the right (the full stop), without [**Shift**], and again depress [**Shift**] while the little finger moves to the right to strike the key for the question mark, as:

```
<>?  <>?  <>?  <>?  <>?  <>?  <>?  <>?
```

The key at the far left of the bottom row produces \ (backslash) and | (vertical bar) with [**Shift**] held down. To type these, use the fourth finger of the left hand, holding down the right [**Shift**] with the fourth finger of the right hand when needed. Practise:

```
a\  A|  \A\  |a|  a\  A|  \A\  |a|
```

## The exercises

In the exercises which follow, do not forget to use the individual shift keys for symbols. In line one of Exercise 17 there is a shift key to type first, then an alpha key and then the symbol.

All the alphabet letters, punctuation marks and miscellaneous characters are included in Exercise 19, which provides excellent practice covering the major part of the keyboard.

Exercise 20 is arranged for [**Caps Lock**] practice, and the lock will have to be released for the typing of the dash (or hyphen) between the items in the list of subjects.

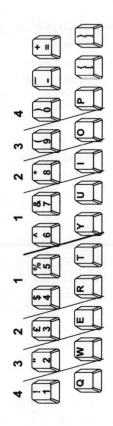

## Exercise 17

1. Aq! :p) Sw" Lo( Def Ki* Fr$ Ju& Gt% Hy^ :p+ ‚ ?:

2. Anne Sue Don Fay Gil Hal Jim Kay Len May Ben Sam

3. Quite Pins Wit Our Eat Idea Rags Urge Tops Yours

4. Jay had a 90% pass in Maths, 95% in French oral.

5. Our Pin Number was "secret" to the bank's files.

6. Janice Hayward & Sons, 34 & 35 Bond Street, Ely.

7. (Please use this letter reference -DERIHLI968).

8. David Lee caught 47 trout and paid £43 for them.

9. Did Mary and Natalie go to 28 Euro Disney shows?

# Exercise 18

**Alphabetic coverage of capital letters**

1. Areas by the Lakeland Park are full of Red Deer.

2. New Zealand is a country for new Olympic Awards.

3. Uncle Fred found a Roman sword at Castle Coombe.

4. Quite a few Western Greek fashions arrive daily.

5. Xerox copies of Val's Intermediate Certificates.

6. Yes, Pearl Divers were saved from the Black Sea.

7. Runnymede is where King John signed Magna Carta.

8. Had Ted negotiated new contracts for Ed and Lee?

9. The Prime Minister met the President of the USA.

**Reminders**: little fingers to operate [Shift] keys; shift key to be fully depressed and held during the striking of the character key.

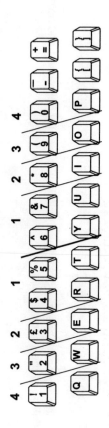

## Exercise 19

1. Bizet & Go offered us this page ( 611 x 8" ) for £9

2. Ted's quotations are: 18/20p or 30/35p per kilo.

3. Please send, by the end of this week, a cheque for £247.

4. Colon (:) and semicolon (;) appear on the one key.

5. Their invoice was for 5 copies @ 65p, less 12%. *

6. Will John send them another copy of this 70p book?

## Exercise 20

Apart from the famous Teach Yourself Typing book the series includes the following:

ASTROLOGY – BIOLOGY – CHEMISTRY – MARKETING – BADMINTON

PHYSICS – ELECTRICITY – INDONESIAN – CROQUET – GEOMETRY

ELECTRONICS – SOCIOLOGY – MATHEMATICS – MUSIC – ALGEBRA

TAXATION – PORTUGUESE – CALCULUS – JAPANESE – ECONOMICS

JAVASCRIPT – PHOTOGRAPHY – SHORTHAND – THE INTERNET

**Reminder**: use the Caps Lock for this exercise.

# Roman numerals

When roman numerals are required, they are compiled from the following letters – capital or small:

```
I=1 V=5 X=10 L=50 C=100 D=500 M=1000
```

Capitals are used for numbers with names of monarchs, chapter headings, acts in plays and books of the Bible, and for numbering paragraphs when it is not convenient to use arabic numerals:

```
Elizabeth II Chapter XX Act I
```

Paragraphs in business letters are usually numbered in lower case, for example:

```
i), ii) and iii)
```

Small letters are also commonly used for numbering the preliminary pages of a book, and for enumerating sub-paragraphs or subsections, scenes in plays or chapters in books:

```
page vi Scene iii I Corinthians iv, 2
```

When working out Roman numerals it is necessary to remember that a letter placed *before* one of greater value indicates that the first number is deducted from the second to find the total, for example, to obtain 40 take X (10) away from L (50) = XL.

A letter placed *after* one of greater value indicates the two are added:

to obtain 60 add X (10) to L (50) = LX;

to obtain 20 add X (10) to X = XX;

to obtain 25 add V (5) to XX (20) = XXV

A line placed over any Roman symbol indicates that its value is multiplied by 1000. Roman numerals should be lined up underneath each other, either to the right or the left.

# Special characters and symbols

There are far more characters available in your word processor than the few dozen that you can see on your keyboard. Those in the extended character sets include foreign letters, mathematical symbols, arrows, bullets and other icons. Characters are stored in fonts, you will find virtually the same set of characters in the main text fonts. The decorative fonts, such as Wingdings, Webdings, Symbol and Monotype Sorts, have very varied sets of characters.

There are three ways in which you can get these characters into Word documents.

## The Symbol dialog box

The first way is the slowest but most reliable:

1　Open the **Insert** menu and select **Symbol…**

2　The **Symbol** dialog box should open with the **Symbols** tab at the front. Browse through the symbols, using the scroll bar to work your way down through the set.

3　For a different set of characters, drop down the **Font** list and select a new font.

4　Click on a character to get an enlarged view of it. (Not in Word XP, which has larger images in the main display.)

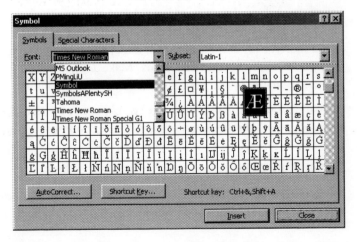

5  When you find the character that you want, click **Insert** to place it into your text.

6  Repeat for more characters, if required, then click **Close** to close the dialog box.

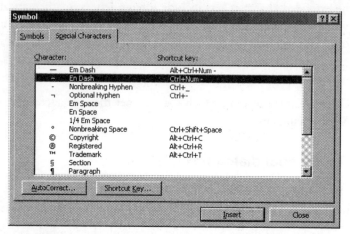

7  For some characters – mainly those used in professional type-setting and document production – you should switch to the **Special Characters** tab. Select the character and click **Insert**.

## Shortcut keys

The second way to insert these characters is to type their *Shortcut key* – a special combination of keystokes that normally includes the [**Ctrl**] key plus one, two or three others. Not all characters have a shortcut key combination, but if they do, they are shown at the bottom of the **Symbol** dialog box. Make a note of those that you use regularly, so that you type the shortcut key in future.

You can create your own shortcut key combination for characters by clicking the **Shortcut Key…** button on the **Symbol** dialog box.

## ASCII numbers

All characters have an ASCII number. (ASCII = the American Standard Code for Information Interchange.) ASCII numbers are the numbers which computers use to represent characters. 'A' for example has the ASCII code 65. You can produce any character by holding down the [Alt] key and typing its ASCII code as a *four-digit number*, e.g. [Alt] + 0169 produces ©. If you omit the 0 at the start, you may get a different character.

The obvious problem of course, as with shortcut keys, is finding and remembering the codes. If a character does not have a shortcut key, its Alt number is shown on the **Symbol** dialog box. Here are a few which you may find worth noting:

| 0149 | • | small bullet | 0153 | ™ | trade mark |
|------|---|--------------|------|---|------------|
| 0169 | © | copyright | 0174 | ® | registered |
| 0176 | ° | degrees | 0188 | ¼ | quarter |
| 0189 | ½ | half | 0190 | ¾ | three-quarters |

Practise! Use the **Symbol** dialog box, then either the shortcut keys or the Alt numbers to insert these characters:

« Æ Ê Ñ ¿ ×

# 08

## speed
## development

# Copying practice

So far there has been graded practice on all four rows of the machine with the object of attaining keyboard mastery, but a good deal of supplementary copying practice will be necessary to complete that mastery. The sense of location will by now be fairly well developed, but regular daily copying practice will produce a noticeable improvement in accuracy and speed.

## Spacing after punctuation signs

In the days of manual typewriters, it was customary to leave one space after a comma, colon or semicolon and two spaces after the full stop, and also after the exclamation mark and question mark. When using a word processor, you should leave a single space after all of these punctuation marks, as the word processor will set appropriate spacing after the ends of sentences. Typing two spaces can produces overlarge gaps, especially in justified text.

When using the hyphen as a dash sign, there should be a space left both before – and after – the hyphen. When "quotation marks", (parentheses) or [square] or {curly} brackets are typed, they should not be separated by any space from the words they enclose.

# Copying exercises

There is no need for the copying practice to be limited to the exercises given here, although these are carefully graded from easy material to more difficult. A section of any book, magazine or newspaper can be used for this purpose. It is useful to practise on a variety of material as this greatly improves speed, accuracy and extends ability.

Practice material is contained in the following exercises. The sentences need to be practised several times individually until a speedy and accurate copy is obtained. When you have decided that you have achieved a satisfactory result at a fast rate, then progress to practising the paragraphs from Exercise 23 onwards. These are graded to enable you to progress so that by the time you reach Exercise 29 you will be able to copy from print any material you require. It is helpful to read through the copy first, then decide on any particularly difficult words, practise these for several lines, followed by any words containing capital letters, or awkward phrases, and then progress to typing the whole paragraph. Where there is difficulty in typing any word, it should be repeatedly typed until that particular letter combination can be copied at a fair rate of speed.

Do not be content with copying the complete exercise once only; each one should be copied several times as repetition of the correct action greatly helps skill and performance. Efforts should be made to slightly increase the speed of typing each time – never put speed before accuracy but try to develop both together. It is useful to remember that a little practice each day is much more beneficial than one long session once in a while!

## Exercise 21

Practise each line until you are sure that you can type accurately and at reasonable speed.

They have arranged to forward this book by parcel post.
See a specialist before you agree to another operation.
We have now seen a full account of the new competition.
If they miss this train they will have an hour to wait.
Please use company letter headings for most of my mail.
They saw another book dealing with short story writing.
He had gone before we were able to check his signature.
During last week many of the men were not able to work.
Use of computers has increased the need to type faster.
We now have to learn foreign languages to visit Europe.

## Exercise 22

A perfect copy is possible when you are a touch typist.

I am pleased to acknowledge the good work done by them.

We are having another machine at the end of the month.

They have taken the house and will be moving in August.

The retail price of butter will be increased next week.

Please co-operate with him as he is having a busy time.

If we add a form it will make a difference to the book.

There is now no doubt about the truth of their remarks.

It will be a pleasure for me to represent this company.

Please send him details of the "Teach Yourself" Series.

## Exercise 23

An agenda is the list showing the order and nature of the business to be transacted at a meeting. Its preparation is usually entrusted to the secretary or to the person responsible for convening the meeting.

Of all the various forms of written communication used in organisations the letter is by far the most common. It provides an essential link between the executives and departments of an organisation and the many external customers, associates and suppliers who are necessary to the successful running of either a business or government department.

Public companies represent the largest type of business organisation other than those owned by the government. They are composed of shareholders who are at liberty to sell their shares publicly without the consent of their fellow shareholders.

In general, a director is one who has the chief management of a scheme, design or undertaking. More particularly, he is one of a number of persons chosen by a majority of the shareholders to conduct the affairs of a company.

## Exercise 24

Book-keeping is the technique of keeping accounts, and recording in a regular, concise and accurate manner the financial transactions of a firm in order to show the financial position at any time.

Dividend is the proportion of profit distributed to the shareholders as a reward for investing in the company. It is expressed either as an amount per share or as a percentage of the nominal value of each share.

An overdraft is the amount of cash which a banker allows his customer to draw out of his bank account in excess of the total balance in the customer's account.

An audit is the official examination of the accounts of a firm to ensure that they are kept in an accurate manner. Laws require the regular inspection of accounting records by auditors.

The Bank of England was suggested by William Paterson, a Scotsman, and it received its charter of incorporation in the year 1694. It was constituted as a joint-stock company with a capital of £1,200,000, that sum being lent at interest to the Government of the day.

## Exercise 25

A good knowledge of at least one European language is essential to obtain the required competence in Business Language skills. It is also necessary to be able to use office equipment in a practical situation. Training involves acquisition of the ability to deal, as a receptionist, with visitors to offices, hotels, hospitals, etc in an efficient, polite and pleasant way.

Modern methods of efficient filing depend on the storage of letters and other documents to preserve them from decay, dirt and damage and, to be easy to use, they must be arranged according to a plan which enables a speedy retrieval afterwards. The plan to be followed must be worked out in sufficient detail to provide an exact and logical place for each letter or document. Ease of reference is just as important as preservation from damage.

On the telephone a person's voice is an important factor and has to stand on its own merits without assistance from any gestures or facial expressions.

Many people who appear to be gracious and lucid in an ordinary conversation seem surly and confused on the telephone.

All people who use the telephone should study the faults they encounter at the other end of the line and try, if possible, to avoid these themselves.

## Exercise 26

FAX is the term used to describe the system of facsimilie telegraphy. This means the instant transmission of printed or drawn items sent via a special copying device incorporated into telephone equipment. Companies are thus enabled to transmit any special letters, documents, photographs, diagrams, etc to many other FAX receivers all over the world as well as throughout Europe.

Business letters are produced today as the result of extensive teamwork. Firstly a graphics designer settles upon a suitable design for the organisation's letterheads. Next an office manager has to decide upon the colour and quality of the paper on which the letterhead will be printed. Many firms take a great deal of trouble over choosing the colours of the paper and letterhead designs and today desk-top publishing can be very helpful. In its final form a perfectly printed copy of the letter is produced on a word processor, and this is then posted. Every discerning company knows that a good combination of design and attractive presentation will go a long way towards persuading the recipient of the letter to accept its message.

While it is easier now to use the many books and visual aids such as posters in learning the spellings of various words, it is not always necessary to wait a whole year to have one's ability tested by an examination. Now it is possible to learn to spell correctly and to be tested at any time by a range of officially verified tests designed to help people judge their own spelling ability. These cover either general vocabulary or are particularly designed for the specialist needs of such areas as medicine or engineering.

This competence is part of the national vocational training developments now available and shows a person's individual assets - very useful when seeking suitable employment. Spelling test achievements can now be listed amongst qualifications in a curriculum vitae of a person's educational achievements and work experience.

## Exercise 27

Many personal Computers now allow the user to create 'templates' for letters, reports, labels and so on into which data from a document or datafile can be inserted. This is also extremely useful in preparing drafts of pages of books which can then be revised, improved and amended as the insertion of new material is easy. A spelling checker is also an important asset. A checker works by going through the pages and locating any word which has been misspelt. It then suggests corrections for the word. Even the most difficult words can be spelt correctly in this way, provided they already exist in the spelling checker's dictionary. Another attractive feature of modern computers is the choice of many different professional fonts or typestyles - these include flowing writing as an option for printing the final edited document.

A legal day is considered to be the whole of the day, continuing up to midnight. When there is a legal obligation to carry out a certain task by a fixed day, the whole day must pass before there can be a 'default'. For example, if rent is payable on a certain day then it is not in arrears until the following day.

An actuary is a person skilled in calculating the value of life annuities and insurances from tables of average mortality rates worked out on mathematical principles. He or she is

also experienced in the preparation of
reports, etc in connection with insurance
matters generally and his or her advice
is called upon in insurance claims
arising from disasters, especially where
any increase in subsequent premiums is
possible.

Shipbrokers are agents – persons or firms
– in a seaport appointed by shipowners to
carry out and perform all the necessary
transactions connected with the business
of their vessels while they are in
harbour, such as entering and clearing
the vessels, collecting freight and so
on.

## Exercise 28

Women have played a crucial literary role throughout history and there are many areas in which women's experiences are now the subject of books.

'Women Heroines of the Second World War' is a book which looks at the lives of ordinary women who fought alongside men in Europe, either in the resistance movements or at home in factories, and on the land. These brave women replaced men in dangerous jobs and often were in the firing line.

Another book has also recently been written about the many achievements of women as healers of all types - midwives, nurses, doctors and campaigners - and this is chronicled throughout the ages. Another has been written about Victorian women who worked down the coal mines and others who organised campaigns to defend the rights of women who worked down the pits.

Books have also been written arguing that the suffrage movement, which resulted in women having the right to vote, helped the cause of democracy in Europe. This is affecting the woman of today in her search for equal job opportunity.

Yet another new book studies the text from women writers of the Middle Ages and pays tribute to their creative talents, aspirations and emotional and intellectual achievements.

Finally a Japanese writer produced a masterpiece during the eleventh century AD with her book - twice the length of War and Peace - and this is still today considered to be a first major work of literature undertaken by a woman.

## Exercise 29

The signs & (and) and @ (at) should never be used in the body of a document as a substitute for the word or words.

The ampersand (&) may only be used in names of companies, street numbers and abbreviations, and the @ sign may only be used in accounts, invoices, price lists, quotations or in e-mail addresses. The per cent sign (%) should only be used when immediately following an arabic numeral.

# 09

# punctuation

# Punctuation marks

Correct punctuation is essential for the production of good type-written work and should be studied carefully. The examples given below show some of the chief uses of the various punctuation marks, which are summarised in alphabetical order at the end of this chapter. Practise the 'typed' part of each section below.

## Apostrophe (')

The apostrophe indicates ownership, a contraction or omission, or plurals of letters and figures. Type a single quotation mark.

**Possessive singular** – add an apostrophe and s ('s):

```
The BBC's programmes.

A typist's chair.

Mrs Brown's typewriter. Mr Sandeman's desk.
Anderson's car.

John's hat and Jane's shoes.
```

**Possessive plural** – add an apostrophe only:

```
Only seven days' notice is required.

Six months' leave was granted. The girls'
hats blew away.

Europe has plans for new theme parks'
locations.
```

But if the plural form does not have an 's', add one to form the possessive:

```
Men's clothes, children's holidays, mice's
ears.
```

**Possessive pronouns** – do not require an apostrophe:

```
This is ours. Where is yours?

The dog wagged its tail. Theirs is in the
corner. She has his and hers.
```

An apostrophe indicates the omission of a letter or letters:

```
Don't it's can't
```

## Comma (,)

The comma denotes the shortest pause or break in continuity:

```
They live in houses, not in huts.

However, it has value. Eurocheques, not
currency, are accepted here. Mary, with her
head in her hands, wept profoundly.
```

Between two long phrases joined by 'and' the comma is often inserted:

```
We thank you for your letter, and have
pleasure in accepting the offer.
```

A short sentence of simple construction does not require commas:

```
I shall go there tomorrow.
```

## Dash (-)

The dash may be used to indicate a break in a sentence. It is used also to separate items, e.g. the contents of chapters in books, and it can precede definitions, explanations and illustrations.

```
There are three kinds of spacing -
character, line and paragraph spacing.
```

When typing the dash leave one space before and after.

If you want to give your document a more professional look, you can use an *en* dash – or the longer *em* dash — so called because they are about as long as the letters 'n' and 'm'. In Word, you can insert them from the **Special characters** tab of the **Insert Symbol** dialog box (see page 59).

## Semicolon (;)

The semicolon indicates a pause in a sentence where the second clause is too closely linked to the first to justify full separation:

```
There has been more than one postponement;
frequent consultations have taken place.
```

The semicolon is also used between clauses of compound sentences:

```
The girls attended the lectures on
fashions; the boys were not interested.
```

## Colon (:)

The colon, although separating parts of a compound sentence. indicates continuity of thought:

```
Be careful how you act: actions speak
louder than words.
```

A longer pause is denoted by the colon rather than by the semi-colon. Important uses of the colon are to introduce quotations, lists, summaries and explanations:

```
The following books are recommended: 'Teach
Yourself Mathematics', 'English for
Business', 'The Pitman Dictionary of
English and Shorthand', 'Teach Yourself
Word'.
```

NB: The lists may be run on or typed in column form.

## Full stop or period (.)

This mark is used to note the end of a complete sentence that is neither a question nor an exclamation:

```
Please reply to our previous letter.
```

The full stop is also used as a decimal point and for time:

```
125.65 £4.20 $59.75 6.00 p.m. 20.45 hrs.
```

Full stops are not now used in modern open punctuation after abbreviations of words and people's names:

```
Dr T Merryweather Mrs E Stopford

Ms T Collins etc eg ie PS UK EEC IMF AGM AD
anon ESc EA Dept CO Exors HMSO FAO IQ Jun
km lb lit lc O&M Messrs TT RID
```

(A comprehensive list of abbreviations and their meanings is to be found at the end of this book. See also page 84 – open and closed punctuation.)

## Ellipses

Full stops are used in groups of three to denote omission of words or an indefinite break – this is called an ellipsis. It can be written as spaced or closed dots:

```
To be continued ...

'Go to the shop . . . and I'll wait for
you.'
```

(In Courier, the font used in these examples, each character occupies the same width and this exaggerates the difference between spaced . . . or closed ... dots.)

The closed dots can be replaced by a special ellipsis character (ASCII 133). In Word, if you type three dots without spacing, they will normally be automatically converted into an ellipsis.

Full stops are used in groups or continuously to guide the eye across a page and are called 'leader' dots. A minimum of one space must be left clear between the last preceding character and the first dot:

```
10 copies ......................... 120p
```

When using tabs to lay out price lists, contents and similar tabulated material, you can attach leader dots to the tabs so that they are produced automatically – see page 151.

# Hyphen (-)

This may show the relationship of two or more words forming a compound word:

```
half-length  self-contained  self-confident
over-enthusiastic  touch-and-go  change-over
shorthand-typist  follow-up
```

The hyphen is also used to mark division of a word at the end of the line of writing (see page 92 for more on hypenation). The modern tendency is to use the hyphen as seldom as possible and many words which were formerly hyphenated (e.g. co-operate) are now written as one word (cooperate).

## Question mark (?)

This is used after a direct question:

```
What is the price of the laptop computer?
```

```
How much shall we pay for a new desktop PC?
```

A question mark is not necessary when an order is given in the form of a question:

```
Will you kindly let us have the information
as soon as possible.
```

## Parenthesis ( )

These are used to enclose subsidiary words, clauses or sentences to explain the leading idea of the sentence:

```
The order (No 3) to which you refer has now
been completed.
```

```
Tinted paper (usually of a cheaper quality)
can be used for specialised copies.
```

Square brackets [ ] are often used to make further enclosure within parentheses, and also for specialised and legal work.

Parentheses should be used sparingly to avoid awkward sentences.

## Quotation marks ( ' , or " ")

Quotation marks, or quotes, are used to enclose words exactly as quoted:

```
'I wish,' he said, 'to express my
gratitude.'
```

The quotation mark should not be placed at the beginning of every line of quoted paragraphs, but only before the first word of each paragraph and at the end of the complete quotation.

The choice of single or double quotes is optional but the style adopted should be used consistently. When a citation occurs within a citation, the alternative form should be used to avoid confusion.

---

### &, @ and %

The signs ampersand (&) and @ (at) should never be used in the body of a document as a substitute for the word or words. The ampersand (&) may only be used in names of companies, street numbers and abbreviations. The sign @ may only be used in accounts, invoices, price lists or quotations, and is normally needed in e-mail addresses. The per cent sign (%) should only be used when immediately following an arabic number.

---

# Capitals

Names of countries, continents, people, months, days, places, book titles and so on are each written with an initial capital letter:

```
England Scotland Wales France Germany
Belgium Holland Italy Spain Greece USA
Canada Peru China Poland Romania Hungary
Europe Asia Africa India Thomas Cook
W Shakespeare Winston Churchill February
March December May Sunday Monday Tuesday
Wednesday San Diego New York San Francisco
Rouen St Helier Brussels Lisbon Madrid
```

```
Cairo Cape Town Teletext Datel Telemessage
Voice mail Videophone Electronic Office
HM Customs Post Office Guide Postal Rates
Overseas Compendium Business Man's Guide
'Teach Yourself Typing' 'Black Beauty'
```

Adjectives derived from proper names will normally be given an intital capital letter:

```
Indian French Revolution American Japanese
```

# Open and closed punctuation

*Open punctuation* refers to the style which uses a minimum of punctuation. This speeds up and simplifies the typist's work, and is most apparent in the omission of full stops after abbreviations.

*Closed punctuation* includes all the punctuation.

The following comparisons show how punctuation marks may be omitted without any loss of clarity.

## Open punctuation

```
We shall expect you at 9 am on Thursday.

Mr J T Smith BSc FRSA

Harry works in the USA.

Please check in at 1500 hrs on Sunday.

Sell all the furniture, ie the tables and
chairs.

This can be paid at any SWEB shop.

PS Greece is a member of the EU.

HRH The Prince of Wales.

Bring all your old toys, etc, to the sale.
```

## Closed punctuation

```
We shall expect you at 9 a.m. on Thursday.
Mr. J. T. Smith, B.Sc., F.R.S.A.

Harry works in the U.S.A.

Please check in at 15.00 hrs. on Sunday.

Sell all the furniture, i.e. the tables and
chairs.

This can be paid at any S.W.E.B. shop.

P.S. Greece is a member of the E.U.

H.R.H. The Prince of Wales.

Bring all your old toys, etc., to the sale.
```

Since open punctuation is now widely accepted, most of the typed examples in the book will follow this style. Whichever method is chosen, it is important to show consistency within a single piece of work.


# Punctuation summary

How to type and when to use:

**Apostrophe**  indicates ownership, omission or contraction of letters and figures.

**Capitals**  use [**Shift**] and release before typing the rest of the word. Can also be used with [**Caps Lock**] for closed capitals, e.g. names of persons, months, days, places, book titles, abbreviations such as BBC, ITV, EU, USA, UNESCO, PTO, STD, PO, PS, RSVP, MC, MP, IQ, HMSO, etc. plus adjectives from proper names, e.g. French Revolution, Indian Mutiny.

**Closed punctuation**  a style of typing which uses full stops after sentences, abbreviations, and uses full punctuation in an addressee's name and address.

**Colon**  separates parts of a compound sentence but on the same theme (see also *dash*).

| | |
|---|---|
| **Comma** | denotes shortest pause or break, and used when joining two long phrases. |
| **Dash** | used to indicate a break in a sentence and to split items, for contents of chapters, or to precede definitions (always leave one space before and after). |
| **Exclamation** | as at the end of sentences – denotes expression of a wish, emotion, or remarkable event. |
| **Full stop mark** | used to note the end of a complete sentence that is neither question nor exclamation. Also used as decimal point, and as an ellipsis to indicate omission of words (use spaced . . . or closed ... dots). |
| **Hyphen** | has no space either side of it and shows two words forming compound word, or used to divide words at line endings. |
| **Open punctuation** | a style which uses a minimum of punctuation, with no full stops after abbreviations, no commas in names, nor in addresses, etc. (see also p. 109). |
| **Parentheses** | (brackets) used to enclose subsidiary phrases – if a second level of brackets is required use { } or []. |
| **Question mark** | used after a direct question. |
| **Quotation mark** | either 'single' or "double" quotes can be used for conversation and for quoting reports of what is actually said. Marks must be placed at beginning of first word of each paragraph then finally *only* at the end of the typing of the complete quotation. |
| **Semicolon** | use when the second part (clause) of a sentence is closely linked to the first part. |

# 10

## formatting documents

# Presentation and layout

Being able to type fast and accurately is a useful and valuable skill, but there is more to producing documents than typing the text. Presentation and layout are very important. Word processors give you the tools to format your documents so that their contents are clearer and more accessible. This chapter introduces the techniques and facilities in Word that allow you to control the appearance of text, and its layout on the page.

# Formatting text

You can set the font, size, style and colour of any amount of text, from a single character to the whole document. Most formatting can be set using the buttons and drop-down lists in the Formatting toolbar, and can be done before or after typing in the text.

To set the formatting before you type, place the insertion point where you want the new text to go – normally at the end of any existing text – and set your formatting options. These will then be applied to everything you type until you change them. To format existing text, select it (see page 7) then set the options.

## Fonts

The font, or typeface, sets the style, shape and – to some extent, the size and weight – of characters. It is therefore the most important aspect of formatting text, and the one that should normally be set before setting the size, or adding bold or other effects.

Fonts can be grouped into three categories:

- Serif fonts have little tails (*serifs*) at the end of the strokes. This makes them easier on the eye, which is why they are often used for large blocks of text. This is Garamond. Other frequently used serif fonts are Times New Roman and **Lucida Bright**.

- Sans serif fonts have simpler lines. They are often used for captions and headings. Examples of sans serif fonts include Arial, Century Gothic and Gill Sans.

- In display fonts, the decorative effect is more important than legibility. They are used for posters, advertisements and the like. Examples are **ALGERIAN**, **Broadway** and Comic Sans.

Some fonts look larger than others. All these examples are the same size (11 points), but see how Lucida Bright or Century Gothic appear bigger than others in their sets. This is why you should always set the font before the size.

You can set the font from the drop-down list on the Formatting toolbar.

1  Select the text to be formatted.

2  Click the ▾ button to the right of the font name to open the list.

3  Select an option from the list.

## Font size

Font size is normally measured in *points*, and 72 points make one inch. Normal text for letters, reports, etc. should be between 10 and 12 point. This text is 11 point.

To set the font size, type the size number in the box or click the ▾ button and select a size from the drop-down list.

## Adding emphasis

If you want to add emphasis to a word, phrase or heading, you can use **bold**, *italics* or <u>underline</u>. These can all be set easily using the buttons on the Formatting toolbar.

1  Select the text to be formatted.

2  Click:  the **B** button to turn **Bold** on

the *I* button to turn *Italics* on

the <u>U</u> button to turn <u>Underline</u> on.

To remove the emphasis, select the text and click the button again.

## Using the Font dialog box

If you want to set several font options at the same time – perhaps to make a heading larger, bold and in a different face – or you want to set one of the less-used options, you can do it through the **Font** dialog box.

This approach is particularly good if you are not sure which font to use, or which settings to apply, as it has a preview pane, which shows you how the text will appear.

1 Select the text to be formatted.
2 Open the **Format** menu and select **Font…**
3 At the **Font** dialog box, click the **Font** tab to bring it to the front.
4 Set the font, style, size and/or other options as required.
5 Check the Preview and adjust the settings if necessary.
6 Click **OK**.

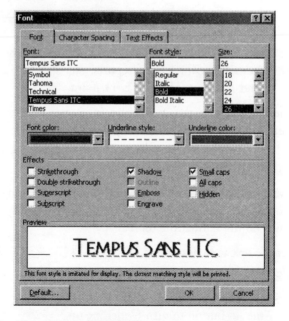

**Figure 10.1** The **Font** dialog box brings together all the options from the Formatting toolbar, plus a range of special effects.

# Paragraph formatting

Some formatting options can only be applied to whole paragraphs. These control the indent and alignment of the text between the margins, and the spacing between lines and between paragraphs.

## Indents

Indents control the position of text between the left and right margins (see page 9), and can be used to make a paragraph stand out from the main body of text. There are three indent settings:

- The left indent sets the distance from the left margin;
- The right indent sets the distance from the right margin;
- The first line indent applies only to the first line. If the rest is indented, it can be a negative value so that the first line starts further to the left than the rest. This is called a *hanging indent*.

> This paragraph has a first line indent of 5 mm. It also has a left indent of 10 mm and a right indent of 10 mm.

This paragraph has a first line indent of –5 mm, to give a hanging indent style

The simplest way to set indents is to use the ruler.

1 If the ruler is not visible, open the **Vew** menu and tick **Ruler**.
2 Select the text to be indented.
3 Click on the indent marker, and drag left or right as required – the dotted line will show you how it will affect the text.

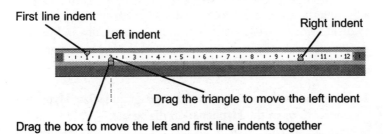

First line indent

Left indent

Right indent

Drag the triangle to move the left indent

Drag the box to move the left and first line indents together

## Justification or alignment

These settings control how the text aligns with the margins – or with the indent, if they are set.

**Left aligned** text is flush with the left margin, but ragged on the right-hand side. Left-aligned is the default in Word. This text is left aligned.

> **Right aligned** text is flush with the right margin. A common example of its use is for the sender's address on a letter.

> **Centre alignment** centres each line between the margins. Headings are often centred.

**Justified** makes the text flush with both margins, for all except the last line of a paragraph. It gives a page a neater look than left alignment, but can create wide gaps between words, especially where the columns are narrow or the text contains long words. This paragraph is justified.

The simplest way to set alignment is to use the toolbar buttons.

1  Select the paragraph(s) to be formatted.
2  Click the appropriate toolbar button.

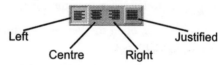

Left        Centre   Right     Justified

## Hyphenation

Where the text is justified, the right edge is made even partly by adjusting the spacing between words and partly by using hyphens to divide words. Word can hyphenate automatically and usually does it very well. If you prefer, you can set the hyphens manually.

**To turn on automatic hyphenation:**

1  Open the **Tools** menu, point to **Language** and select **Hyphenation...** to open the **Hyphenation** dialog box.
2  Tick the **Automatically hyphenate document** checkbox.
3  Click **OK**.

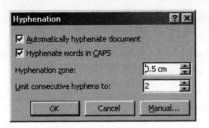

**To set hyphens manually:**

1 Open the **Hyphenation** dialog box.

2 Click **Manual…**

3 When a word is to be split, you will be prompted. Click **Yes** to accept the hyphenation, or **No** to leave the word intact.

If required, you can turn off hyphenation for text.

1 Select the paragraphs.

2 Open the **Format** menu, select **Paragraphs** and on the **Line and Page Breaks** tab, tick **Don't hyphenate**.

## Hyphenation guidelines

If you want to set your own hyphens, follow these guidelines:

1 A word of one syllable or its plural should not be divided.

2 Hyphenated words should be divided at the existing hyphen.

3 Compound words may be divided at point of juncture.

4 A word may be divided after a prefix or before a suffix, provided that a two-letter division does not result.

5 A person's initials should not be separated from the surname – the forename should follow the title and may be separated in this instance from the surname.

6 A divided word should not end a paragraph or page.

7  A word should not be divided in such a way that pronunciation of either half is affected.

8  Words containing double consonants may usually be divided between those consonants.

9  Words containing three consecutive consonants may be divided after the first consonant.

10 If in doubt as to the correct point of division, do not divide.

## Line spacing

Word allows you to set the spacing between the lines. There are three depths of spacing in common use: *single* (no additional space between the lines), *double* (one blank line between each line of text) and *treble* (two line spaces between each line of text). These three forms are shown in Exercise 30.

To set the line spacing:

1  Open the **Format** menu and select **Paragraph...**

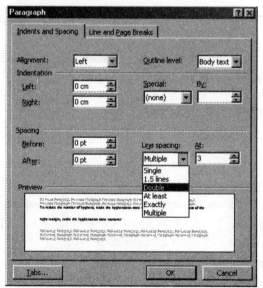

**Figure 10.2** The **Paragraph** dialog box – note that Single, Double and Multiple are not the only line spacing options. Explore the others when you have a few spare moments.

2 On the **Indents and Spacing** tab, open the **Line spacing** list.

3 For *single* or *double* spacing, select the setting from the list.

4 For treble spacing, select *Multiple* from the list, then set the **At:** value to 3.

## Spacing between paragraphs

You can set the spacing between paragraphs by specifying the gap to leave before and/or after a paragraph. Setting one of these to 12 point is equivalent to putting a blank line (of normal text size) between paragraphs, but thinner or wider spacing can be used as required.

If you want to separate paragraphs by a standard-width blank line, just press [**Enter**] twice after each paragraph – once to end it, and once to make an extra line.

If you want to adjust the spacing in any other way, it can only be done through the **Paragraph** dialog box.

1 Select the paragraph(s).

2 Open the **Format** menu and select **Paragraph...**

3 On the **Indents and Spacing** tab, open the **Line spacing:** drop-down list and select the level.

4 For spacing between paragraphs, set the **Before** or **After** values – enter a new value or click the arrows to move it up or down.

---

### Format before or after

When you type, the text will be formatted with the current settings. This means that you can set the alignment, line spacing and other options when you first start a document, and those settings will be applied to the text as you type it. To format or reformat existing text, select it then set the format options.

## Exercise 30

Single-line spacing is generally used for
long letters, invoices, tabular
statements, poetry, synopses, footnotes,
minutes and lengthy documents. If a
double line space is needed between
paragraphs press the [Enter] key twice at
the end of the paragraph.

Double-line spacing is used for short

letters, lecture notes, literary work,

essays, sermons, legal documents and

dialogue in plays.

Treble-line spacing is used for drafts,

and for literary and legal work which may

need revision.

**Tip:** Where a different line spacing is to be applied to one or two
paragraphs in a larger document – as in this exercise – it is
probably simpler to type the entire text first, then go back and
select and format the paragraphs.

# Templates

A template is a document which has some formatting and fixed elements in place when it is first opened. An obvious example is headed stationery. This would have the firm's name, address and other contact details at the top, perhaps accompanied by a logo, and the formats would have been set so that text automatically appears in the chosen font, size and alignment. A more advanced template might also have the date, and allocated and formatted places for the recipient's details, the salutation and other elements, so that all letters followed the same layout and style.

Word comes supplied with a range of templates for many different kinds of documents. You can also create your own templates – and in a business, you would normally expect to use one set up with the company's details and formatted to the company's house style. All templates – Word's and those that have been created – are normally stored in the same folder, and accessed the same way.

**To start from a template in Word 98 or 2000:**

1 Open the **File** menu and select **New**.
2 The **New** dialog box contains several sets of templates. Click on a name tab to bring that set to the front.

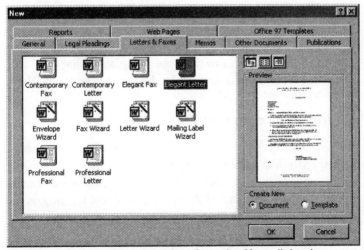

**Figure 10.3** Selecting a template from the **New** dialog box.

3 Click on a template to see its preview.
4 When you find a suitable template, click **OK**.
5 Replace the prompts with your own details and other text.

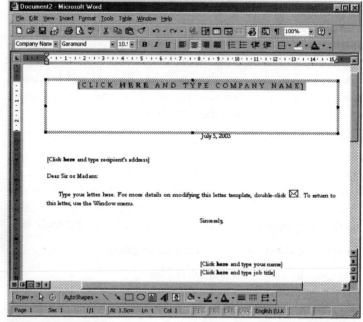

**Figure 10.4** Word's own templates often have allocated and ready-formatted places for specific items. These are marked by prompts.

In Word XP, **File > New** will open the **New document Task Pane**. Select **General templates** to open the **Template** dialog box. This is the same as the **New** dialog box in the earlier versions of Word.

## Making your own templates

You can create your own templates for everything from headed notepaper to draft contracts. Set up a document with a suitable design and layout and all the fixed information, but leave out any specific details – the name of the person, the quote for the job, the text of the letter, and so forth – then save it as a template.

1 Starting from a template or blank document, enter the fixed text and other items.

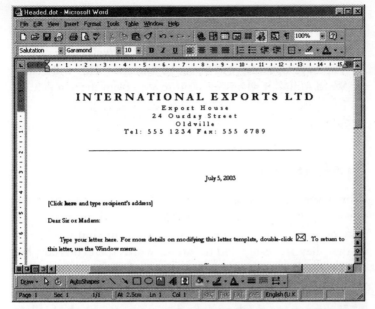

**Figure 10.5** A template based on Word's *Elegant Letter* template. This has simply had the firm's details added.

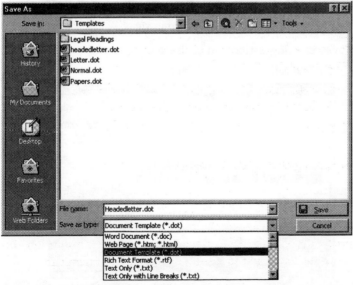

**Figure 10.6** The **Save As** dialog box when creating a template.

2  Open the **File** menu and select **Save As…**

3  Click the arrow to the right of the **Save as type** slot to drop down the list of types. Select *Document template*.

4  The **Save in** folder will be set to *Templates*. This will enable Word to find it when you want to start from the template.

5  Enter a filename – it will be given the extension *.dot*.

6  Click **Save**.

# Spell checking

Word's spell checker has a good dictionary, but this does not cover everything. Proper names, technical and unusual words may be seen as errors. These can be added to your dictionary, so that they are recognised in future. Words spelt correctly, but used wrongly, e.g. 'there' when you needed 'their' are not picked up by the spell checker, but should be by the grammar checker.

1  If you want to check *part* of a document, or a block of cells in a spreadsheet, select it.

2  Open the **Tools** menu and select **Spelling** or click 📖.

When a word is not recognised you can:

♦  Select a **Suggestion** and click **Change**.

♦  If it is a valid word click **Ignore**.

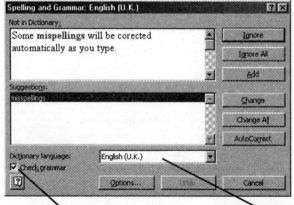

Do you also want it to check your grammar?     Which dictionary?

- Click **Add** to put it in a custom dictionary.
- Click into the text, edit the word then click **Change**.

Word has a check-as-you-type option, which will highlight mistakes as you make them. This can be distracting. You may prefer to just run a spell check after you have finished.

**To change the spelling options:**

1  Open the **Tools** menu and select **Options…**

2  Click the **Spelling & Grammar** tab to bring it to the front.

   An option is turned on if its checkbox is ticked.

3  Click the option text, e.g. **Check spelling as you type**, or its checkbox to turn the option *on*, or *off* if it is already on.

4  If you turn the grammar check on, you should select a **Writing style**. In an office, this should be set to Standard or Formal.

   In the XP versions of Word, you can specify which aspects of grammar and style to check.

5  Click **OK** to close the dialog box when you have finished.

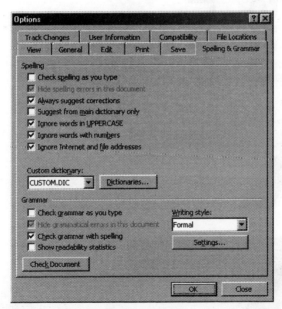

**Figure 10.7** Setting the Spelling & Grammar options.

# 11 business correspondence

# Business letters

The letter is by far the most common form of written communication used by organisations, and these letters will convey their messages more effectively if they are attractively produced.

The chief characteristics of a good letter are clearness, accuracy, brevity and courtesy. There are various components of a business letter, and in the paragraphs that follow each part is explained in full, i.e. letter headings, references, date, name and address of the addressee (the person or firm to whom the letter is being sent), the salutation (Dear Sir, etc.), subject heading (if any), the body of the letter, continuation sheets (if necessary), complimentary close, the title (designation) of the sender (if any), enclosures and envelopes.

For your own portfolio you may wish to include some of the business letters given at the end of this chapter as examples that you have personally produced.

## Sizes of letter paper

The standard size of business letter paper is A4 (210 mm × 297 mm). For very short letters and private (personal) correspondence you can use A5 size (210 mm x 148 mm). Both sizes can be used in either portrait or landscape orientation (see page 10).

### Width of margins

Margin widths are governed largely by individual preference and the length of the letter. The margins should be set before starting work. A minimum left margin of 25 mm is generally recommended for A4 paper, however, with a slightly narrower margin for A5.

Modern practice is to allow even left and right margins to secure a centred effect on the paper, in much the same way as the printed page of a book.

# The components of a business letter

## Letter headings

These headings are generally the product of the graphics designer and are carefully prepared since they play an important part in projecting the desired corporate image. The details given in the letter heading include, in bold display type, the name and business of the firm, the company's registered address from which that business is conducted, company number (as applicable), telephone, telex and/or FAX numbers, etc. For private correspondence the heading usually only contains the address and telephone number.

Professionally-printed headed paper is used where the heading is in colour or has an embossed design. If the heading can be produced with the office printers, letter documents should be started from a template which contains the heading design (see page 97).

## Insertion of date

The order recommended is day, month (spelled out in full) and year typed on one line, as:

```
17 April 20-- or 17th April, 20--
```

Start the date at the left-hand margin point when adopting the *fully blocked* style, or align it to the right when using the *indented* or *semi-blocked* style of layout.

## Reference initials

In business correspondence these references usually consist of the initials of the dictator and the typist, as DF/OH or DF/oh. Alternatively, a departmental number may be used, as SALES/916. If a place has not been allotted for these details in the printed letter heading or template, they can be placed at the left-hand margin, as shown in the examples on pages 110 and 117. Sometimes the initials are inserted at the end of the letter.

When replying to a correspondent, do not forget to include his or her reference. It will be helpful to him or her in dealing with the letter – that is the reason for its insertion.

## Attention line

When instructions are given that correspondence must be addressed to a firm and not to individuals, it is common practice to insert an 'attention line', e.g.

```
FOR THE ATTENTION OF MR J HARMAN
```

This should be placed two line spaces above the inside address (see page 109).

For the layout of an attention line on an envelope, see page 112.

## Inside name and address

The name and address of the person or firm to whom the letter is being sent are in most cases placed at the beginning of the letter. Single spacing should be used, with all lines beginning at the left-hand margin. It is common practice to type the inside address in the same form as the envelope address (see pages 111–112), with the post town in capital letters. Every care should be taken to ensure that the name of the correspondent is given correctly.

## Personal, private, confidential

When it is desired for a specific reason to restrict the reading of the letter to one particular person, the words giving the instruction should be typed, preferably in capitals, two line spaces above the inside address.

## Salutation

The opening to a letter is termed the 'salutation', and the most common forms used include:

```
Dear Sir Dear Mrs Jones Dear Mr Smith

Dear Sirs Dear Madam Dear Ms Black
```

Type the salutation two or three line spaces below the inside address.

## Subject heading

When a subject heading is required it should be typed two line spaces below the salutation and aligned to the left or centred over the writing line. Unless the heading ends with an abbreviation, a full stop should not be inserted after it. The heading may be formatted in bold or italics to give it emphasis.

## Body of letter

This contains the subject matter of the letter. It should commence two line spaces below the subject heading, or below the salutation if there is no heading. Paragraphs may be blocked or indented according to the letter style. Single-line spacing with an additional line space between paragraphs is preferable, but double spacing throughout is sometimes used for short, one-paragraph letters.

Do not use the ampersand (&) for 'and' in the body of the letter, unless reference is made to the name of a firm or street numbers are being quoted.

## Insets

These are paragraphs that are displayed within the body of the letter. If the paragraphs are numbered or lettered, two or three spaces should be left after the number or letter or its closing bracket.

Inset paragraphs may be blocked, indented or hanging. When the blocked method of layout is being used, inset matter can begin at the left-hand margin. Otherwise, paragraphs should be indented equally from both margins. In hanging paragraphs the first line overhangs the second and subsequent lines by two spaces.

A line space should always be used between the text and the inset material, and, unless the items are very short, between paragraphs in the portion inset.

## Continuation sheets

These are needed when a letter occupies more than one sheet and should be of the same size as the headed letter. Continuation sheets are not usually printed with the heading. The details required on the continuation sheet are the page number, date and the addressee. The company name should be added where this helps to identify the addressee.

When the fully blocked style of letter layout is used, the details are listed separately at the left-hand margin:

```
2
17 April 20--
R Kelly Esq, Green Bros
```

With the indented method, the information is evenly displayed across one line with the page number in the centre:

```
R. Kelly, Esq.   Green Bros(2)   17th April, 20--
```

Do not use a continuation sheet for only two lines. Adjusting the margins may make it possible to fit the letter on one sheet.

## Complimentary close

This is typed two line spaces below the final paragraph of the letter and should begin at the left-hand margin or the middle of the line of writing. Those most used are:

```
Yours sincerely Yours truly

Yours faithfully
```

The form of the close should match the salutation – 'Yours faithfully' with 'Dear Sir', but 'Yours sincerely' with 'Dear Mr Smith'.

## Name of the firm or company

Capital letters are used if the name of the company follows the complimentary close, and the letter may be signed by a member of the staff who acts as an agent.

The name of the firm may be prefaced by 'for'. The abbreviated form of *per procurationem* – **per pro.** or **p.p.** – is also used.

## The signature

This will be handwritten, and, when the designation of the writer is placed after the complimentary close, a minimum of five line spaces should be left for the insertion of the signature. The designation should be typed at the left-hand margin, or be centred under, or commence at the same point as, the complimentary close when the indented or semi-blocked style of layout is used.

## Enclosures

The indication of enclosures to a letter is given by typing the abbreviation, *Enc* or *2 Encs* in the space that may be provided for this information or at the bottom left-hand corner of the letter. (If there is room, *Enc* should be typed two or three line spaces below the designation.) Labels are sometimes affixed to the letter and a duplicate placed on the enclosure.

## Layout

On page 109 the suggested layout for an open punctuated, fully blocked letter is given in diagrammatic form, together with a key to the sections. On page 110 an example of an open punctuated, fully blocked letter with subject heading is given. You will find, however, when working in an office, that the company has its own decided views and rules on house- style with regard to spacings, layout and so on.

## Copies and backup files

For business purposes it is desirable to have a record of documents despatched. In some situations a physical copy of the document will be required, in others a file on disk will be sufficient. It is essential that file names identify documents clearly. A simple but effective system is to use the recipient's name or reference code and the date, e.g. *SmithBros090703.doc*. Files should be organised so that documents can be retrieved quickly. There might be folders for each client, for each area of the business, or for each type of document. Depending upon the quantity of documents, you may need to subdivide folders. The essential requirement is that there should not be more than a few dozen documents in any one folder.

Backup copies are also essential. Computer systems and their hard disks do fail sometimes; files do get erased by mistake. A file is only safe if there is at least one more copy of it on another disk or tape, stored separately from the computer. If the computer is burnt, stolen or otherwise lost, the records must still be available if the business is to continue trading.

**LETTERHEADING**
**Name & address of firm**
**plus telephone and FAX numbers**

Line
space:

| | | |
|---|---|---|
| 1 | **Our ref** | uses initials of writer, oblique/then typist, e.g. HM/LK |
| 0 | **Your ref** | e.g. LMS/DFB |
| 1 | **Date** | Day, month in words and then year e.g. 7 March 200- |
| 1 | **Any special instructions** | PERSONAL, PRIVATE & CONFIDENTIAL, URGENT, FOR THE ATTENTION OF |
| 1 | **Name and address of addressee** | Start at margin for fully blocked fresh line for post town in CAPS. Post code is on last line - 1 space between 2 parts of code, e.g. Miss L M Sewell 56 Bell Lane EASTBOURNE BN21 lLJ |
| 1 | **Salutation** | Dear… |
| 1 | **Subject heading** | Use UPPER CASE and/or **BOLD** |
| 1 | **Body of letter** | Always leave one clear line between paragraphs |
| 1 | **Complimentary close** | e.g. Yours faithfully (with Dear Sir) Yours sincerely (with Dear Mr, Miss) |
| 0 | **Name of firm** | (if applicable), e.g. Yours faithfully JOHNSON & SONS PLC |
| 4 | **Name of person signing letter** | Sometimes Mr, Miss, Ms is put after name, e.g. Helen Miller (Miss) |
| 0 | **Title of person** | e.g. Managing Director |
| 1 | **Enc** | No full stop in open punctuation |

**Figure 11.1** Example of a fully blocked business letter

*Remember to start with each line at the left-hand margin*

**WRITERS IN STYLE P L C**
**Westbourne House Bushey Heath**
**Herts WD25 6PY**

Telephone 08100950 005778                    FAX 08100950 005888
(2)
Our ref  HM/LK
Your ref LMS/DFB
( 2 )
7 March 200-
(2)
PERSONAL
(2)
Miss L M Sewell
56 Bell Lane
EASTBOURNE
BN21 lLJ
(2)
Dear Madam
(2)
FULLY BLOCKED BUSINESS OR PERSONAL LETTERS
(2)
I am writing to let you know how easy it is to obtain a neat, efficient appearance
in any business or personal letter by using the above fully blocked style of
display.
(2)
You will see that one line space is left between the reference, date, special
instruction line, addressee's name and address and the salutation, etc. in fact the
only place that there is need for more space to be left is when typing the
complimentary close and the name of the person signing the letter (called the
signatory). You need to leave four clear line spaces for the signature. Finally, one
clear line is left between the title of the person and any enclosure to be sent with
the letter.
(2)
I hope that you will find this information as useful as I did when I started typing
business letters. I also enclose one of our brochures on 'New Job Opportunities
in Writing' which I think you will enjoy reading.
(2)
Yours faithfully
WRITERS IN STYLE PLC
(5)
Helen Miller (Miss) Managing Director
(2)
enc

**Figure 11.2**  Example of an open-punctuated fully blocked style,
with subject heading. Note: The numbers between the parts of
the letter show the number of times to press [Enter].

# Envelope addressing

When typing envelopes it is necessary to remember to include:

| | |
|---|---|
| Person or company name | Miss L A H Owens |
| House no., building name (if any), street | 29 Birchwood Mews |
| local description of area (if supplied) | Whitstone |
| TOWN NAME (in BLOCK CAPS) | TALGARTH |
| County (in lower case with initial cap) | Brecon |
| Postcode | LD3 4DT |
| Country | Wales |

The usual guide on where to begin printing the address on an envelope is to start about halfway down from the top edge so as to leave 4 cm for postage stamps and a postmark. Indent from the left-hand side approximately 4 to 5 cm, the name and address being roughly centred. Almost all companies now incorporate fully blocked style into addresses (see examples below).

Note that except for large towns like London, the county is included on a separate line and the Post Office also prefer the postal code to be on a separate line.

Commonly used sizes for envelopes:

> C 6 (114 mm x 162 mm)
>
> C5/6 (110 mm x 222 mm)

Addresses are usually typed in single spacing, but double spacing may be used for large envelopes or if the address is very short.

Courtesy titles, such as *Mrs, Mr, Dr, Ms, The Rev* should always be included with the name. *Messrs* is sometimes used when addressing a partnership, except when the name of the firm is preceded by the word *The* or a title is included (examples: *Messrs Brown &Jones, Messrs Avis & Co*, but *The Regent Manufacturing Co, Sir James Smith & Co*). A limited company is an incorporated body – a legal person, distinct from any of its members – so that *Messrs* is strictly out of place when used before its name, although if personal names are included, *Messrs* is sometimes used in practice.

Initials representing forenames should always be followed by a space, but degrees and complimentary initials after a name, such as *MA, BSc, MBE,* are not divided by a space.

Supplementary notes placed on the envelope, such as *Personal, Urgent,* etc, should be typed two line spaces above the name. Internal instructions, such as *First Class,* may be typed in the top left-hand corner.

When *Junior* and *Senior* are required (father and son with the same first name and at the same address) the abbreviations *(Jun* or *Sen)* are placed immediately after the name, as *Mr Arthur Carey Jun* or *Arthur Carey Jun Esq.*

Examples of addresses are given below, and in Exercise 31 a list of names and addresses (all fictitious) are provided for practice. A folded sheet of paper, or any scrap of paper with an area similar to an ordinary envelope, will be suitable for practice

---

Sir James Brown & Sons Ltd
345 Rochester Road
CHATHAM
Kent
CH9 2SB

---

FOR THE ATTENTION OF MR. J. SMITH
Messrs. James Melhish & Co. Ltd.,
546 Caledonian Road,
BIRMINGHAM.
B9 5TX

---

**Figure 11.3** Examples of block form of address. (Note that in the second address the punctuation is 'closed'.)

Type these addresses in block form with open punctuation.

Dr John Brown, 36 Dudley Road, Derby DE6 2LX

Messrs S W Kemp & Sons, 26-30 Booth Street,
Northampton NN5 5LT

Mr Robert Macdonald, 145 Ladywood Road,
Portsmouth PO1 5RJ

Major Herbert Wilson DSO, Bridge Avenue,
Reading, Berks RG4 OAZ

Professor Sir Albert Lawrence, Melville
Lodge, Coventry CV1 3AN
*(Show that this letter is confidential)*

J N C Allerton Esq, 29 Whitmore Road,
Plymouth PL3 5LU

E Griffiths & Co Ltd, Exeter Street,
Newmarket NE7 1NJ

Ms Wendy Odell, 63 Charlton Hill, Chester
CH1 4JN

Mrs A Freeman, J Freeman & Sons Ltd,
Compton Road, Bournemouth BH8 9NG
*(Show that the letter is personal)*

Mr Robert Grant Jun, Belmont Road, Falmouth
FA9 2XC

F T Pemberton & Co Ltd, 42-48 Ashley Road,
Dover, Kent DO9 6SP

The Rev William Gardner MA, The Rectory,
Grange Road, Norwich NO8 5RM

Type these addresses in block form with closed punctuation.

The Bridge Manufacturing Co. Ltd.,
Claremont Road, Gloucester. GL1 5PH

Mrs. Elsie Davidson, 29 Stapleton Road,
Greenwich, London. SE13 5NB

# Memorandums

The memorandum is used for internal communications only, i.e. between members of the same organisation. A memorandum (or memo) form is usually A5 (landscape), although A4 may be used for longer memos.

The heading 'Memorandum' is printed at the top of the page. There is no salutation or closure, but spaces are provided for the sender's and recipient's designations or names, the date, the subject and possibly the reference. The subject heading may be typed at the left-hand margin or centred. A left-hand margin of 25 mm (1 inch) should be allowed, unless the memo is aligned with the printed matter at the top, which may be less than 25 mm from the edge of the paper.

---

MEMORANDUM

To Sales Representative

From Buying Manager                                    3 October 200-


CHRISTMAS NOVELTIES

The new catalogue of Christmas Novelties is now available. Please let me know as soon as possible how many copies you will require for distribution to your customers.



EMW/JW

---

**Figure 11.4** Specimen layout for a memorandum

These are used for business or personal correspondence when the message to be conveyed is short. The recipient's address is typed on the front and the message on the reverse side. Most business firms have their name and address printed on their postcards, but a typed address should be confined to one line if possible and may be separated from the text by a continuous line. As in the case of memos, there is no salutation or closure. Postcards are normally A6 (148 mm x 105 mm) and margins of 1.5 cm to 2.5 cm should be allowed depending on the length of the message.

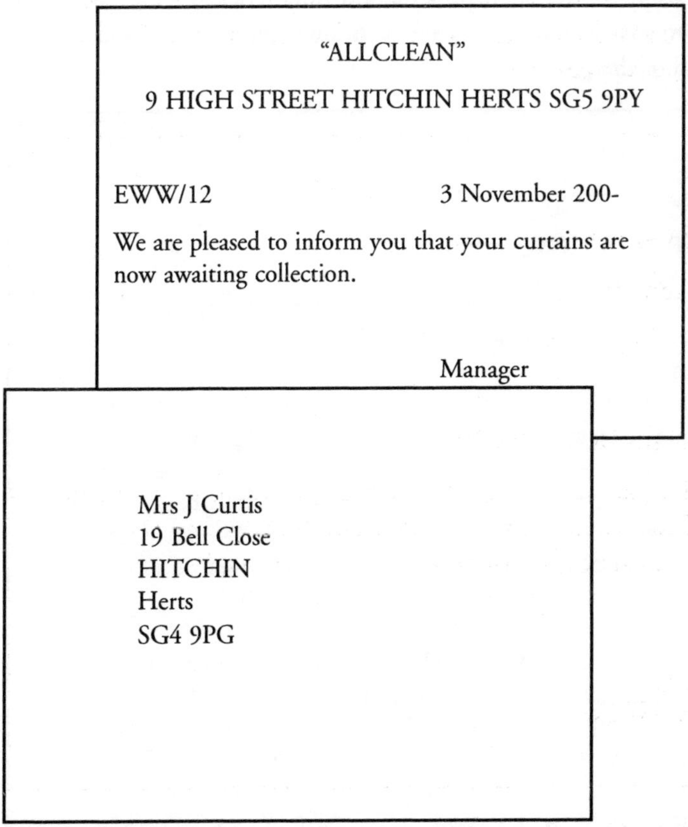

"ALLCLEAN"

9 HIGH STREET HITCHIN HERTS SG5 9PY

EWW/12                                    3 November 200-

We are pleased to inform you that your curtains are now awaiting collection.

Manager

Mrs J Curtis
19 Bell Close
HITCHIN
Herts
SG4 9PG

**Figure 11.5**  Specimen layout for a postcard

# Linked themes

On the following pages there are examples of business letters, memoranda and personal business letters. These are incorporated into sets of correspondence on linked themes. The theme is a set of correspondence between various people and firms linked by a logical progressive sequence of events.

## Exercise 32

### Layout of internal memorandum

Example of an open punctuation fully-blocked style memorandum with heading. Compose your own reference and add it at the end of the page.

```
M E M O

TO      All staff (2)
FROM    Managing Director (2)
DATE    23 August 200- (2)
SUBJECT SPOT THE ERROR COMPETITION
        PRIZEWINNER
2)
We have now scrutinised all the entries for
the above competition - we received 239,327
in all - and found that only one person
correctly located the 1,439 errors in the
manuscript. This is Miss B L Cross and I
have today written to notify her and to
send her the cheque for £12,000.
(2)
There will naturally be a release to the
press concerning our winner and I am
holding the special Press Conference on
Monday at 1100 hours. Everyone should be
present to maximise the coverage and I need
not stress to you all that Miss Cross's
home address and telephone number must be
```

kept entirely confidential. From a
telephone conversation I had with her, I
gather she plans shortly to have a holiday
in Devon with a friend who has been ill,
and after that to go abroad (following the
official presentation) which may help her
to avoid the inevitable considerable
publicity.
(2)
Thank you all for your help in what has
been - for this Company - a most worthwhile
competition. We +raised a total of £120,000
for the WWAW Fund, and the Company has been
personally thanked by the European
President of that Fund.

## Exercise 33

**Layout of a fully blocked letter**

Example of an open-punctuation fully blocked style letter with
heading. Choose suitable margins and type a copy of this business
letter, then type an envelope.

**WORLD WIDE PUBLISHING PLC**
**MASON'S COURT CROMWELL WAY**
**BIRMINGHAM B5 9WS**
TEL 0121 2789 453576          FAX  0121 2789 453354

Your ref
Our ref BLC/23/ED

23 August 200-

Miss B L Cross
22 Little Heath Close
Muswell Hill
LONDON
N10 8UK

Dear Miss Cross

**COMPETITION PRIZE - TENTH ANNIVERSARY**

We are writing to inform you that you have been awarded first prize in our SPOT THE ERROR competition run in conjunction with the Medwater Publishing Company, and commemorating our Tenth Anniversary as publishers.

Your entry correctly located the 1,439 errors in the manuscript of the book published and entitled 'Keep the World Greener'. Yours was the only entry that successfully detected all the deliberate mistakes. We wish to congratulate you on this outstanding achievement and enclose a cheque for £12,000 made out in your name. Please acknowledge and return our official receipt in the enclosed self-addressed envelope.

We hope that you will be able to fulfil some life-long ambition by winning this competition.

Our publicity department will wish to take some photographs of you, with your permission, and will be contacting you shortly.

Yours sincerely
WORLD WIDE PUBLISHING PLC


Managing Director
encs

## Exercise 34

Use A5 plain paper (landscape) for this receipt and attach it to the letter to Miss B L Cross.

```
RECEIPT

To WORLD WIDE PUBLISHING PLC

(in conjunction with Medwater Publishing Co)

I HEREBY ACKNOWLEDGE RECEIPT OF CHEQUE FOR
£12,000 (TWELVE THOUSAND POUNDS) BEING THE
SUM AWARDED TO ME FOR FIRST PRIZE IN THE
TENTH ANNIVERSARY COMPETITION.

Signed.....................

Date  ................20..

(Belinda L Cross)
```

Read through the rest of the series of linked correspondence in this section, then type perfect copies of each as follows:

**Exercise 35**: Letter from Miss Cross to her friend Miss Daphne Mortimer.

**Exercise 36**: Letter from Miss Cross to the Managing Director of World Wide Publishing PLC thanking him for sending the cheque.

**Exercise 37**: Letter from Miss Cross to Mr W Richardson, Bank Manager of Barcham's Bank PLC concerning investment of money.

**Exercise 38**: Mr Richardson's reply to Miss Cross.

**Exercise 39**: Memo from Mr Richardson to Kevin Millhouse. *Remember:*

- in each letter or memo you must choose your own suitable margins and ensure that A4 sized paper is used unless specific instructions are given to the contrary;

- this correspondence must be mailable (i.e. free from errors) and ready for signature in each case.

### Exercise 35

This is an example of *indented* style of letter. Note the alternative position of the addressee's name and address. You may also omit the addressee's name and address in personal letters of this type.

Set a first line indent of 10 mm. Type an envelope.

---

                        22 Little Heath Close
                        Muswell Hill
                        LONDON N10 8UK

Telephone 0208 806749  2 September 200-

Dear Daphne

    I am writing to let you know the good news that I have just received from World Wide Publishing PLC.

    As you may remember, I entered a competition in their magazine to spot the manuscript errors in an author's book which was shortly to be published. It was all about the environment and was entitled 'Keep the World Greener'. The Company has just written to say that I have won First Prize and they also enclosed their cheque for £12,000!

    The first thing I have decided to do is to pay for a holiday in California for both of us. I know that when I went there with Jane and Thelma last year you would have been very eager to come if you had been able to do so. This is now your chance to see America. As you have been so exhausted since that last bout of influenza, I think a few days away in Devon in the very near future will be a tonic for both of us.

    Shall I go ahead and book the flights and accommodation for San Diego and a

suitable hotel on Dartmoor? We can easily
manage this year to stay in a five-star
hotel. Please telephone to let me know your
decision as soon as possible, and send a
list of convenient dates for the holidays.

   Best wishes

            Yours sincerely


Miss Daphne Mortimer
67 Tether Lane
Crews Hill
ENFIELD
Middx

## Exercise 36

Set suitable margins. Type a copy of this letter and an envelope.

                              22 Little Heath Close
                              Muswell Hill
                              LONDON

Telephone 0208 806 749

Your ref BLC/23/ED

2 September 200-

The Managing Director
World Wide Publishing PLC
Mason's Court
Cromwell Way
BIRMINGHAM B5 9WS

Dear Sir

COMPETITION PRIZE - TENTH ANNIVERSARY

Thank you for your letter of the 23 August
200- informing me that I have won first

prize in the above and enclosing your
Company's cheque for £12,000. I now return
your official receipt, which I have duly
signed and dated.

I am extremely grateful to your Company for
so kindly organising this competition in
aid of the World Well Animal Wildlife Fund.
The fact that I have won first prize will
enable me to help a friend who has been ill
to benefit from two exciting holidays in
the near future.

I have no objection to my photograph being
given to the press.

Yours faithfully


Belinda L Cross (Miss)

enc

## Exercise 37

Set suitable margins. Type a copy of this letter and an envelope.

22 Little Heath Close
Muswell Hill
LONDON

Telephone 0208 806 749

Your ref KG/RTD/2998/wr/ls

16 September 200-

Mr W Richardson
Barcham's Bank PLC
High Street
ELMS END
Cambs
CB3 1DR

Dear Mr Richardson

I am writing to enquire whether you could help me with some investment advice.

Recently I have been fortunate enough to win a considerable sum of money as a result of entering and winning the Spot the Error Competition held in aid of the WWAW Fund. I now need to have some advice on how to invest this in an appropriate account to give the maximum return each month. As I shall be using some of the money for a holiday in the USA, I will also need to order some travellers' cheques and currency from your bank.

Can you tell me please how much notice you require for currency (dollars) and for travellers' cheques to be prepared?

An early reply from you will be much appreciated as I plan to leave for the USA around 25 October.

Yours sincerely


Belinda L Cross (Miss)

## Exercise 38

---

# BARCHAM'S BANK PLC

### HIGH STREET
### ELMS END CAMBS CB3 IDR

Telephone: 0353666882                    Fax: 034478934

Our ref KG/RTD/2998/wr/ls

18 September 200-

Miss B L Cross
22 Little Heath Close
Muswell Hill
London N10 8UK

Dear Miss Cross

Thank you for your letter of 16 September
concerning investment possibilities.

I was very pleased to hear about your
admirable success in winning the
competition and I am sure that it must have
taken a great deal of skill to detect all
the errors in that manuscript. It so
happens that I also endeavoured to discover
them when the competition was run and only
succeeded in finding about 800! From what I
have just read in the Press, you discovered
1,439 which was excellent.

1) I am enclosing a brochure of our latest
profile plan which I am sure you will find
interesting. I am also asking our
Securities expert, Kevin Millhouse, to
prepare a special set of options for you to
look at including any tax free investments
that you may wish to make.

2) Perhaps you would be good enough to look
through the enclosed papers and also
discuss the set of options with Kevin

Millhouse. Afterwards you can book an appointment to discuss in detail with me what you have decided to do.

3) As regards your holiday, the bank requires only a minimum of three working days for the ordering of currency but we do keep travellers' cheques in stock all the time, so you can obtain these when you collect your currency.

Yours sincerely


Manager

enc

### Exercise 39

Set suitable margins and type a copy of this fully blocked memo.

Include reference WR/KG/RTD/2998.

Use your own template or copy the one below.

```
M E M O

TO        Kevin Millhouse Securities

FROM      William Richardson

DATE      17 September 200-

SUBJECT CLIENT INVESTMENT ADVICE

I have been asked by one of our clients to
provide an investment portfolio for a
considerable sum of money which she wishes
to invest to obtain maximum return on
capital. I thought you would be able to
arrange a plan for her. Looking at my
records I find that she is 39 years old and
anticipates retiring at age 60.

When I telephoned this client she informed
me that she intends to invest about £8,500.
Are there any tax-free investments that she
can make?

Please look upon this as a matter of
urgency as she is going on holiday in
October.
```

# Meetings

## Notice of a meeting and agenda

This should be sent out well in advance to all those entitled to attend. It states the day, time, place and purpose of the meeting.

An agenda is a list of topics to be discussed at a meeting. These should be arranged in local order with the routine business first.

---

```
THE AXON CAR CLUB

The Third Annual General Meeting of the
Axon Car Club will be held at the Royal
Hotel, Broxbourne, on Sunday 5 October
200- at 1500 hours.

AGENDA

1 Minutes of last meeting.

2 Treasurer's report.

3 Membership fees.

4 Election of new members.

5 Date of next meeting.

6 Any other business.



J Stevens
Secretary


Highbourne House
Park Street
Broxbourne, Herts.
12 September 200-
```

---

**Figure 11.6** Specimen layout for a combined notice and agenda

## Chairman's agenda

In a chairman's agenda the items listed for discussion are typed down the left-hand side of the page, leaving the right-hand side blank for the chairman's notes. A left-hand margin of 25 mm should be allowed. A minimum of treble-line spacing should be allowed for each item. An example appears below.

```
THE AXON CAR CLUB

AGENDA FOR THE THIRD ANNUAL GENERAL MEETING

To be held at the Royal Hotel, Broxbourne,
on Sunday 5 October 200-

1 Minutes of the
last meeting.


2 Treasurer's Report.


3 Membership Fees.


4 Election of new
committee members.


5 Date of next meeting.


6 Any other business.
```

**Figure 11.7** Specimen layout for a chairman's agenda

# Minutes

Minutes of a meeting are the official record of the proceedings of that meeting and are generally printed on A4 paper. The heading always contains the name of the club, firm or society, and the date, time and place of the meeting, and is followed by a list of those present. The items are dealt with in the order that they have been presented on the agenda. Each item is numbered and has a heading.

```
THE AXON CAR CLUB

MINUTES OF THIRD ANNUAL GENERAL MEETING

Held at the Royal Hotel, Broxbourne, on

Sunday 5 October 200- at 1500 hours.

Present: Mr John Price, Chairman
         Mr James Price, Vice-Chairman
         Mr P Brown
         Mr James Stevens, Secretary
         Mrs P Smith
         Miss L Jackson
         Mr K R Frost
         Mr B Bacon
         Mr Alan Green, Treasurer
         Mr S P Brown

1  MINUTES OF PREVIOUS MEETING

   The Minutes of the second Annual General
   Meeting held on 3 October 19— were read,
   approved and signed.

2  TREASURER'S REPORT

   Mr Alan Green reported that the balance
   of Cash in Hand and at the Bank was in a
   healthy state and bearing in mind the
   proposed outlay for a new photocopier
   and additional stationery supplied, the
```

**Figure 11.8**   Specimen layout for minutes of a meeting

financial position of the Club could be regarded as very satisfactory.

3 MEMBERSHIP FEES

It was unanimously decided that the membership fee should be increased by £1.50 to £10.50.

4 ELECTION OF NEW MEMBERS

Mr Alan Brown and Miss Jill Noble were duly elected members of the club.

5 DATE OF NEXT MEETING

The date of the next meeting was fixed for Sunday 3 December 200-.

6 ANY OTHER BUSINESS

The question of time, place and date of next year's Rally was raised and it was decided to postpone any decision until the next monthly meeting.

Chairman

December 200-

# 12

## deciphering manuscript

# Working from handwritten copy

So far all of the copying practice has been from typewritten examples or printed matter but one of the typist's tasks is to decipher manuscript.

The best way of preparing to type from a handwritten original script is first to read through a fairly lengthy section. This will enable you to get to know and understand the writer's style and handwriting, and to become familiar with and understand the subject material. When there is any difficulty in understanding a word, print a draft leaving a space where the unreadable words are placed and it may be possible subsequently to fill in the correct word when you get to know the writer's style and are conversant with the content.

Drafts can be printed in double-line spacing to allow room for corrections. Treble-line spacing is generally used for legal drafts as they may undergo extensive revision by each party before being ready for signature.

# Correction signs

Drafts of letters and documents contain alterations in the margins, and corrections are also made to the contents.

| Sign in text | Sign in margin | Meaning |
| --- | --- | --- |
| ⅄ | # | insert space |
| ⌒ | | close up space |
| - - - - - - | *stet* ✓ | where a word has been crossed out, the dotted line and *stet* (let it stand) or a *tick* mean 'ignore the crossing out signs' |
| / | | cross through word(s) or letter to be altered |
| ⊢——⊣ | ૧ | remove words completely |

| Sign in text | Sign in margin | Meaning |
|---|---|---|
| ⋏ | /in our opinion/ | insert items written in margin at this point (correction can also be put in balloon with arrow to where it is to be inserted in text) |
| // or [ | NP | new paragraph |
| ⌐ | | run on (no new paragraph) |
| ( ) | trs | transpose vertically (change over position of words or lines) |
| ⌐ or ↺ | trs | transpose horizontally (change over position of words or lines) |
| ≡ | caps | change to capital letter(s) |
| ≢ | l.c. | change from capitals to lower case |

You will find that some instructions or alterations to drafts are contained in hand-drawn balloons and these are usually placed in the margin nearest to the word or phrase to be changed.

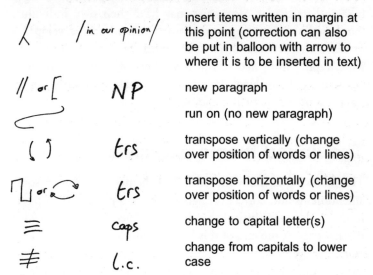

Unusual or unreadable words in the text are made clearer by words (usually printed in capitals for clarity) which are placed within a dotted box in the margin.

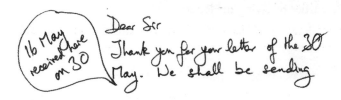

There are several variations in the form which correction signs take and particular companies may have their own individual 'house styles' when using corrections. The writer also develops his or her own particular style so the most important thing to do when typing from manuscript is to check with the person who has written the original draft to ensure that you clearly understand his or her particular marks.

## The linked theme exercises

The following exercises are on linked themes and contain some amendments and correction signs. They also provide the opportunity to decipher difficult handwriting. There are keys provided to each page at the end of this book to enable you to check your work.

The work on linked themes is more interesting for the person typing the correspondence. (It is now usual for NVQ examinations to take the form of correspondence and documents on linked-theme work. The typist is then able to understand the build-up of the correspondence and the resulting action that is taken by any of the parties receiving the letters, etc.)

# Abbreviations

While a more comprehensive list of abbreviations is to be found on pages 180–185, some simple examples are given here and these should be typed in full in the final copy of the document. The first 15 are frequently used, the next 12 being more used in business and European contexts.

| Abbreviation | Meaning |
|---|---|
| abt | about |
| aftn | afternoon |
| asap | as soon as possible |
| asst | assistant |
| bn | been |
| plse | please |
| sh | shall |
| shd | should |
| wk(s) | week(s) |
| wh | which |
| wd | would |
| wl | will |
| yr(s) | your(s) or year(s) |
| ea | each |
| ffy/ffly | faithfully |
| AGM | annual general meeting |
| ETA | estimated time of arrival |
| ETD | estimated time of departure |
| EU | European Union |
| O/D | overdraft/overdrawn |
| FAO | for the attention of |
| HO | head office |
| IMF | International Monetary Fund |
| kg | kilogram |
| km | kilometre(s) |
| VAT | Value Added Tax |
| P & L | Profit and Loss |

# Exercise 40

HOME ADDRESS

Today's Date

Westoby & Sheerwater PLC
369 Church Street Gardens
EDMONTON
N9 7YT

Dear Sirs

POST AS PERSONAL ADMINISTRATOR — PERSONNEL DEPT

I am enclosing my application form for *(ABBREVIATIONS IN FULL)* the above post in yr Co.

Should I be fortunate enought to be ~~eventually~~ considered as a possible candidate I would be able to attend an interview at any time to suit you except on ———————— when I have trs to attend a *Glasgow* conference in on behalf of my company.

stet ✓ Yours ~~faithfully~~ —

(YOUR OWN NAME)
etc

*(Key on page 187)*

## Exercise 41

Use your own name, details and experience to complete this form after you have printed it. The position for which you are applying is Personal Assistant/Administrator in the Personnel Department. Sign and date the form.

WESTOBY & SHEERWATER PLC
369 Church St Gdns
EDMONTON    N9 7YT    → *Centre each line*

*Bold, caps* JOB APPLICATION FORM

Title of Job .............. Dept ...........

APPLICANT'S FULL NAME (BLOCK CAPITALS)

SURNAME .............. FIRST NAMES ..........

ADDRESS .............. 
.............. POSTCODE ..........

DATE OF BIRTH .............. NATIONALITY ..........

EDUCATIONAL QUALIFICATIONS (Please give dates)

*bold* School .............. 
..............

*bold* College ..............

*bold* Other ..............

*bold* ~~Typing~~ Speed (if applicable) ..... WPM

EXPERIENCE (Please give dates)

*bold x3* Job Title        Company        Dates

..............
..............

*bold* Salary Required .............. p.a.

REASONS FOR APPLYING FOR THIS POST

..............
..............

Signed .............. Date ..........

*(Key on page 188)*

## Exercise 42

### Jonathan Henry Miller & Sons PLC

ESTATE AGENTS
9 WEST FRONT
CAMBRIDGE CB1 8DR

Tel 01223 686 00777          Fax 01223 686 44335

Our ref DM/JR/BEECH
Date

q  Mr & F R Finlay                    [HORRINGER]

/Dr/  Roves Cottage [High St [Horringer [IP32 1QR  (NPx3)

Dr Mr Finlay

[all caps]  re purchase of flat at 15 Beech Mews E9 3XL
[no underline]
9 am writing to ~~confirm say~~ th 9 have put forward ✓

q  yr offer of £195,600 to Mrs Baine, ~~she is~~ the

/the/  vendor. She has accepted ~~her that~~ with the

[proviso!]  proviso th, as the figure is lower than the

[not]  asking price of £205,000, she is/prepared to

include the new carpets, curtains and light

NP  fittings in the sale. [Please let me know

as soon as possible what your views are.

Yours sincerely

DOROTHY MILLER
Manager

*(Key on page 189)*

## Exercise 43

Set out the following business letter with suitable spacings. Type these abbreviations in full:

& = and, only remains in abbreviated form in address

w = with

max = maximum

yr(s) = your/yours or year(s)

Gen Man = General Manager

---

(Reference)

(Today's date)                    *use open punctuation (ie no commas)*

Mr J W Webb, ⌈Chief Design Engineer, ⌈Messrs John Smith & Company, ⌈901 London Road, ⌈MAIDSTONE, MA5 6LR

Dear Mr Webb

Owing to the steady growth of our business we are moving to larger premises in Main Street, Slough, Bucks at the end of this month. The site is a particularly good one, in the heart of this industrial centre, within easy reach of London & the M4 Motorway. The transport difficulties which we have experienced in the past will now be reduced to a minimum, & early deliveries ensured. The new factory will be fully automated w a resulting increase in both the quality & quantity of our output.

We trust that you will be patient w us during this transitional period. Any delays should be minimal only & we expect to achieve max production again within five weeks.

May we take this opportunity of expressing our thanks for yr confidence in the past & we hope that the improvements we shall introduce will lead to even more business.

Yrs sinc ⟋ *leave 4 clear line spaces*
J Simpson
Gen Man

# Exercise 44

## *Jonathan Henry Miller & Sons PLC*

ESTATE AGENTS
9 WEST FRONT
CAMBRIDGE CB1 8DR

Tel 01223 686 00777          Fax 01223 686 44335

Our ref SJ/

DR FREDERIC AVE¥
10 BIRCH AVENUE,
CHURCH STREET,
EDMONTON, N9 9XV

} *use lower case with initial caps except use caps for EDMONTON*

Dear . . . . . DR AVEY

SALE OF 10 BIRCH AVENUE CHURCH STREET, EDMONTON N9 9XV THE THATCHED COTTAGE, LYLE LANE, GODMANTON, CAMBRIDGE CB19 1BR

(✓) We are pleased to advise you that we have placed an advertisement photograph in a local paper with a large distribution area offering your property for sale at the agreed price of £49,000 159000 (check price from list).

The paper will be published on friday of this week and we anticipate a good response to our advertising advertisement. std (✓)

[ If we receive any offers for your

property, we shall immediately contact you and take instructions regarding the sale. It is always advisable to be prepared to accept an offer if this falls within your financial expectation, and we have priced your property at a suitable figure to enable you to do this.

If we can be of any further assistance, please do not hesitate to contact us. In the meantime we will continue to show prospective purchasers round your property.

Yours sincerely

SANDRA JOHNSON
PROPERTY CONSULTANT — to be with initial caps

*(Key on page 190)*

## Exercise 45

Decipher and type this memo, incorporating the printed details given below opposite.

MEMORANDUM

TO   Sandra Johnson, Property Consultant

FROM   Natalie Miller, Executive Director

MARGIN
1¼"
APPROX

MARGIN
1" APPROX

DATE

~~SUBJECT~~ ADVERTISEMENTS FOR NEW PROPERTIES

I am sending you the 3 latest advertisements which we need to publish in the

uc     "huntingdon and cambridge Weekly Herald"

NP     this week. // Please check ~~that~~ that

*/     all the details are correct price, description, etc and then notify the

lc     Clients that we are advertising (these) properties for sale as from next

uc     friday's edition. // The photographs NP are arriving from the processors

✓ ⊙   ~~today~~ tomorrow   I think you will find that the "Herald" needs to have our advertisements (four) days before publication. ⌐

Run on (This is a new ~~expanding~~ growing local

trs     paper with a distribution which

corress a

h ✓ /wide area around Cambridge and
Huntingdon and we should have some
good response to our (advert.) IN FULL

close up //I would appreciate any comments on
potential improvements etc which you
tns       may wish to make as I (feel sometimes)
that our descriptions of properties
more /   could be /dynamic and (appealling.)
                                    ? spelling

INSERT A

NP [Please let me know as soon as
you have organised this and ~~and~~
send me a copy of the PROOFS

*(Key on page 191)*

(A)

1) Deceptively spacious thatched cottage with good
sized grounds, situated in quiet village opposite
church - 3 beds, 2 rec, garage, stable block and
barn. £250,000. Ref QD 46. (GODMASTON)

2) Beautifully refurbished detached house in sem-
rural position with large gardens, garage, 3 beds,
large kitchen. *£232,000*. Ref QD 47. (CLAYTONBURY)

3) Just reduced for quick sale - 4 bed terraced
Georgian house in city centre, 3 reception rooms,
off-street parking for 3 cars, short distance from
river (mooring rights also available) £260,000.
Ref QD 48. (CAMBRIDGE)

THE PROPERTY LETTING CENTRE
Head Office: 24 Lynton Close   Elm End Rd
                                WATFORD   WD3 7KM
(in full) Our ref: BKCM/ht          Telephone 0923 1200099
         4 Sept 200-                        FAX 0923 1226565
Mr D A V Jackson
Avenida de Alvarode
Vascenceles  2993
2711 SINTRA
Portugal

Dear Mr Jackson

Re: 15 Beechwood Mews, Harewood St, Potters Bar

Further to our visit at the above flat on 31 Aug
200-, we now pleased to confirm that, as agreed,
we have placed property details of the on our
books at a charge of £520 per calendar month.
As you are aware, the rental income will be
inclusive of maintenance, ground rent, rate for
which you are currently responsible. The
services such as Gas, Telephone and Electricity
will be payable by the Tenants and they will
be informed by us to sign for the supply
prior to their occupation.
We always advertise our properties only to Professional
Persons and we take up their references on your
behalf. A deposit of one month's rental plus 100
booking fee is paid to us plus the one month's
rental in advance. We then deduct our fees from
this sum and forward to you an account

plus the balance of the monies due to you. Nixon

    If you require any alteration to this
uc arrangement, ie for this company to pay
the monies into an English bank account
on your behalf we shall be pleased to do
this for you. [It may be that you will
find ~~that~~ you will need to make use of our
lc Full Property Management Service whilst
you are staying for an indefinite period
abroad, and, if you ~~should~~ require any
further information, please ~~do~~ not
hesitate to contact ~~this~~ ~~Company~~. stet Nixon

INDEFINITE

In the meantime I enclose our brochure
containing details of the full management
service we provide.

Yours Sincerely

WENDY MACPHERSON
Property Letting
Manager

enc

*(Key on page 192)*

# Exercise 47

Type a copy of this brochure to send with the letter to Mr Jackson.

[Centre] [ALL CAPS] THE PROPERTY LETTING CENTRE

this brochure is to give you information regarding
our two services of property letting. Both services
include a free valuation of your property/to [by our expert
ascertain that a correct rental is to be charged. valuer]

[CAPS] The first, which is a full management service,
guarantees that this company will find you a suitable
professional person to rent your property for six
monthly (or one yearly) periods. The Company takes up
full financial and personal references on your behalf
and collects the rents as and when/due. A full [these become]
tenancy shorthold/agreement is drawn up and signed by
both parties. The full management service means that
you have space and peace of mind as/should any
repairs etc become necessary/the company arranges for
the appropriate/to be worked carried out, and debits
your a/c accordingly. This is a particularly suitable
service for owners who are too busy to supervise the
lettings personally or who are living abroad. there [CAPS]
is a charge of 12 per cent for this service.

[bold] We offer the second service which is a part
management service where this Company guarantees to
find a suitable professional person to rent your
property for six monthly or one yearly periods. The
Company takes up full financial and personal
references on y/our behalf and collects the rents as
and when due. A full tenancy agreement is drawn up [CAPS x2]
and signed by/both parties/this is a suitable [© CAPS
service for owners who are able to/supervise the [personally]
letting personally and arrange their own repairs.
There is a charge of 10 per cent for this service.
Should you require to change over from the part
management service to full management at any time
during the tenancy/this can be arranged at a fee of [period]
two per cent extra.

[s/ CAPS] In both service/the tenant will be asked to provide a
deposit of/one month's rental/in advance and to pay [italic
his or her rent by standing order at a bank or
through a building society. [trs]

*(Key on page 194)*

# Exercise 48

Before starting this exercise read carefully through and learn the following abbreviations. These must be typed in full in the letter.

Sep = September, ref = reference, advert = advertisement, shl = shall, wl = will, poss = possible, & = and, wrk = work, Oct = October, wd = would, St = Street, max = maximum, mnth = month, m/c = machine, htg = heating, wrkd = worked, yr = your (or year), Yrs = Yours, fthfly = faithfully.

---

24 Sep 200-

The Manager

Property Letting Centre

245 Lynton Close

Elm End Road

WATFORD   WD3 7KM

35 Egatt Barnes Ave /s

Dykes Bury   MIDDLESBROUGH

Cleveland

NT3 7LK

Telephone No 0642 /224439 ⁸⁷

Dear sir

With ref to your advert in today's edition of the 'Daily provincial and Cleveland Echo', I shl be grateful if you wl kindly send me as soon as poss details of the 2 flats you have available – ref nos numbers G789 and G901.   G

I am commencing wrk in central london on 10 Oct and am urgently in need of a fully furnished 2 bedroom flat near to a railway station that wd be convenient for commuting to Liverpool St station.

The max rental I am prepared to pay is £180 per week or £750 per calendar month mnth.

[The flat must have an automatic washing m/c, tumble dryer, fridge, freezer, cooker extractor hood, & some form of central htg. I do also need good parking facilities to be available nearby, preferably on the premises.

[In order to save time I am enclosing the names and addresses of 2 referees to whom you can write and you will note that one is my employer in Middlesbrough for whom I have wrkd for 5 years.

[I plan to visit London on 26 Sep and, if I like the flat after viewing it, I shl be prepared to sign a contract immediately and move in on 30 Sep or as soon after that date as is poss.

Thank you for yr help in this matter.

Yrs ffthfly

Belinda Richardson (Miss)

enc

*(Key on page 195)*

# 13 tabular work

# Tabs

Tabs are used to align text vertically. If you are writing a price list, CV or other document where text or figures need to be in accurate columns, you can use tabs. By default, the tabs are at 1.2 cm (½ inch) intervals and left aligned – when you enter your text or numbers the left edge is at the tab position. The position and the style of the tabs can be easily changed. Tabs can be aligned to the left, right, centre, or to a decimal point, or they can draw a bar.

When you press the [**Tab**] key, the insertion point moves to the next tab stop position. The text that you type there will be aligned according to the tab style.

### Tab styles

Left edge of the text aligns with the tab.

Text centres on the tab.

Right edge of the text aligns with the tab – use this to align whole numbers.

Decimal points align with the tab – use this to align currency and other numbers with decimal fractions.

Bar tab draws a vertical line at the tab point.

### Setting tabs

Like all formatting, tabs can be set before you type the text or afterwards. If you know exactly where the tab stops are required, then they can be put into place first and the text will visibly fall into columns as you type. If you are not sure of the layout, type the first few lines, then set the tabs. As you click each new tab into place, the text will be aligned with it, and you can adjust the tab stop positions to give the best layout across the page. The rest of the text can then be typed.

**To set tabs using the ruler:**

1  If the ruler is not present, open the **View** menu and tick **Ruler**.

2  Select the text for which you want to set tab stops.

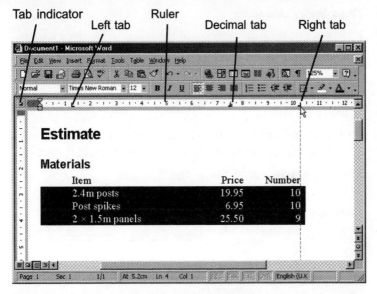

Tab indicator   Left tab   Ruler   Decimal tab   Right tab

**Figure 13.1** Setting tab stops using the ruler.

3   The current tab style is shown at the left of the ruler. To change the style, keep clicking the icon until you see the style you want.

4   Click on the ruler to place the tab stop. The default ½ inch interval tabs to its left will be removed.

5   To move a tab stop, click on it and drag it into its new place.

6   Repeat steps 3 to 4 to set any other tab stops for the selected block of text.

7   Click anywhere in the working area to clear the highlight from the text.

If necessary, the positions of tab stops can be adjusted at any time – simply reselect the text and drag the stop across the ruler.

## Leader characters

If the columns are not close together, you can set leader characters – dots or a solid line – on a tab to guide the eye across from one item to the next. They can be set through the **Tabs** dialog box.

**To set leader characters:**

1 Make a note of the position of the tab(s) to be given leaders.

2 Open the **Format** menu and select **Tabs...**

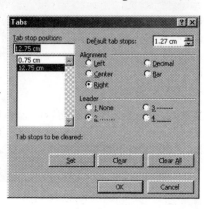

3 At the **Tabs** dialog box, select the tab stop.

4 Select the **Leader** style – dots, dashes or solid line.

5 Click **Set** to apply the style.

6 Repeat steps 3 to 6 to set a leader on another tab.

7 Click **OK**.

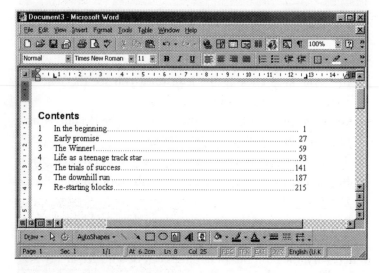

**Figure 13.2** Leader characters set on a tab.

**Tip:** If you want to create a dotted line on a form, set a tab stop with a dotted leader. You do not need to type any text at the tab stop.

# Tables

Tables offer an alternative way to lay out data in neat columns. Use them instead of tabs where you want to draw borders around the blocks of text, or to have coloured backgrounds to some or the rows or columns, or where the items are too large to fit on one line at a tab stop. (But note that you must use tabs if you want to set leader characters.)

You should set up the table before you start to type its text. It does not matter if you do not know exactly how big the table needs to be. Rows and columns can be easily added if they are needed.

**To create a simple table:**

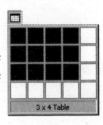

1   Place the cursor where the table is to go.

2   Click and drag the highlight across the grid to set the size. Carry on and drag *off* the grid to make a table larger than 4 x 5.

Or

3   Open the **Table** menu, point to **Insert** and select **Table**.

4   Enter the number of columns and rows.

5   Set the **AutoFit** option:

*Fixed column width* makes all the columns the same width.

*AutoFit to contents* adjusts the widths – as data is entered – according to how much data is in each column.

*AutoFit to window* stretches the table so that it fills the width of the page.

6   Click **OK**.

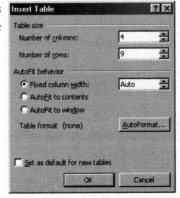

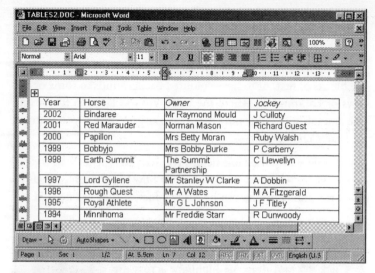

| Year | Horse | Owner | Jockey |
|------|-------|-------|--------|
| 2002 | Bindaree | Mr Raymond Mould | J Culloty |
| 2001 | Red Marauder | Norman Mason | Richard Guest |
| 2000 | Papillon | Mrs Betty Moran | Ruby Walsh |
| 1999 | Bobbyjo | Mrs Bobby Burke | P Carberry |
| 1998 | Earth Summit | The Summit Partnership | C Llewellyn |
| 1997 | Lord Gyllene | Mr Stanley W Clarke | A Dobbin |
| 1996 | Rough Quest | Mr A Wates | M A Fitzgerald |
| 1995 | Royal Athlete | Mr G L Johnson | J F Titley |
| 1994 | Minnihoma | Mr Freddie Starr | R Dunwoody |

**Figure 13.3** In a table, if the data item at any one point is too big to fit in the column, it will be wrapped round onto a second line. Where tabs are used for layout, a large item may overrun into the next column, pushing the rest of the line out of alignment.

## Lines and borders

When a table is first created, it has thin lines between the rows and columns, and around its outer border. You can remove or redefine these lines and borders.

1  Click on the ⊞ icon that appears at the top left when the cursor is in the table. This selects the whole table.

2  Right-click and select **Borders and Shading…** from the menu.

3  Select the **Setting** – *None* (clear all lines); *Box* (outside border); *All* (grid and box); *Grid* (inside lines) or *Custom* (lines selected and formatted separately).

4  Select a **Style** from the list. It will then be applied to whichever lines are selected in the Setting option.

5  Select the **Color** and **Width**, to apply to the selected lines.

6  Click **OK**.

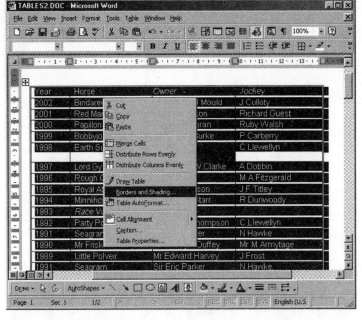

**Figure 13.4** Starting to format the lines of a table. The table has been selected and the menu opened with a right-click.

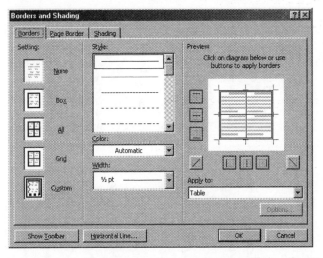

**Figure 13.5** The **Borders and Shading** dialog box. The Style, Color and Width are applied to the lines selected under Setting.

## Exercise 49

### List of Subjects

| | | |
|---|---|---|
| Accountancy | Dietetics | Mathematics | Printing |
| Advertising | Economics | Metallurgy | Refrigeration |
| Aeronautics | Elocution | Mineralogy | Salesmanship |
| Architecture | Engineering | Mining | Shipping |
| Arithmetic | English | Music | Shorthand |
| Banking | First-Aid | Needlework | Sociology |
| Book-keeping | Geography | Optics | Telecommunications |
| Building | History | Pharmacy | Television |
| Calculations | Insurance | Photography | Theatre |
| Chemistry | Investment | Physics | Transport |
| Commerce | Journalism | Poetry | Typewriting |

(Key on page 197)

**Exercise 50**

Type this list of US Presidents, using these tabs: Name = left; Party = centre; Dates = right.

| Ref | Name | Party | Dates |
|-----|------|-------|-------|
| 1 | Eisenhower, Dwight | Rep | 1953–61 |
| 2 | Kennedy, John F. | Dem | 1961–63 |
| 3 | Johnson, Lyndon | Rep | 1963–69 |
| 4 | Nixon, Richard | Rep | 1969–74 |
| 5 | Ford, Gerald | Rep | 1974–77 |
| 6 | Carter, Jimmy | Dem | 1977–81 |
| 7 | Reagan, Ronald | Rep | 1981–89 |
| 8 | Bush, George H.W. | Rep | 1989–93 |
| 9 | Clinton, William J. | Dem | 1993–2001 |
| 10 | Bush, George W. | Rep | 2001–present |

If the columns have headings, the same tab stops are normally used for the headings and the data. The exception is right- or decimal-aligned numbers, where different tabs will usually be set to centre the headings.

## Exercise 51

Type this list of Grand National winners, first using tabs to produce four left-aligned columns, then create a new 4 by 14 table and type the text into its cells. When you have typed each data item, press [Tab] to move to the next cell in the table.

| Year | Horse | Owner | Jockey |
|------|-------|-------|--------|
| 2002 | Bindaree | Mr Raymond Mould | J Culloty |
| 2001 | Red Marauder | Norman Mason | Richard Guest |
| 2000 | Papillon | Mrs Betty Moran | Ruby Walsh |
| 1999 | Bobbyjo | Mrs Bobby Burke | P Carberry |
| 1998 | Earth Summit | The Summit Partnership | C Llewellyn |
| 1997 | Lord Gyllene | Mr Stanley W Clarke | A Dobbin |
| 1996 | Rough Quest | Mr A Wates | M A Fitzgerald |
| 1995 | Royal Athlete | Mr G L Johnson | J F Titley |
| 1994 | Minnihoma | Mr Freddie Starr | R Dunwoody |
| 1993 | Race Void | | |
| 1992 | Party Politics | Mrs David Thompson | C Llewellyn |
| 1991 | Seagram | Sir Eric Parker | N Hawke |

**Exercise 52**

Electra Machine
Quarterly Sales

| Branch | March | June | Sept | Dec |
|---|---|---|---|---|
| Southampton | 136 | 210 | 195 | 187 |
| Portsmouth | 125 | 167 | 154 | 170 |
| Liverpool | 103 | 141 | 139 | 126 |
| Birmingham | 214 | 230 | 179 | 223 |
| Manchester | 212 | 176 | 194 | 182 |
| Leeds | 317 | 265 | 276 | 284 |
| Sheffield | 284 | 314 | 237 | 350 |
| Burnley | 147 | 201 | 169 | 229 |
| Middlesbrough | 231 | 198 | 217 | 186 |
| Cardiff | 246 | 312 | 256 | 306 |
| Swansea | 193 | 224 | 184 | 219 |
| Newport | 231 | 189 | 209 | 196 |
| Totals | 2,439 | 2,627 | 2,409 | 2,636 |

(Key on page 198)

## Exercise 53

Use the decimal tab to align the number values in this currency conversion table.

| Country | Currency | Rate per £1 |
| --- | --- | --- |
| EU | Euro | 1.44 |
| Australia | Dollar | 2.49 |
| Brazil | Reai | 4.66 |
| Fiji | Dollar | 3.06 |
| Hong Kong | Dollar | 12.72 |
| India | Rupee | 75.32 |
| Japan | Yen | 192.12 |
| Mexico | Peso | 17.10 |
| Russia | Rouble | 49.52 |
| South Africa | Rand | 12.43 |
| Turkey | Lira | 2,302,403.83 |
| United States | Dollar | 1.63 |

# 14

## speed tests

# Repetition practice

It may not be within the capacity of every typist to attain a championship rate, but regular practice on the exercises in the earlier sections should have secured a fair speed of operation. High speed will not be attained unless the touch system has been mastered; the eyes must be kept on the copy throughout the test.

One of the most helpful methods for increasing speed is repetition on straightforward printed matter, which should be typed and retyped several times. The matter selected should be varied, and suitable pieces can be found in any book, magazine or newspaper; small print, however, should be avoided. The repetition practice should be abandoned immediately there is any question of partial memorisation and a new piece should then be selected.

# Strokes and words

When the question of typewriting skill is being discussed it is usually in terms of ability to type at so many words a minute, but it is not generally understood that the *word*, in this context, is a measured unit. It would not be reasonable for two lengthy words to have the same time value as two short words. For example, take 'terminological inexactitude' instead of 'untruth'. In the first rendering there are 27 strokes or depressions of keys, including the space bar, and in the second there are only seven keystrokes.

The usual method of counting takes an average of *five* keystrokes for each word. Each time a key is depressed, whether it is a character key, punctuation or the space bar, it counts as one stroke.

# Speed test practice

1   Obtain an electronic timer such as a clock or watch with alarm facility, or an electric timer from a hardware store. This is needed to set a time, say three minutes to begin with, then progressing to five minutes as your speed and accuracy develops. Finally, a

ten-minute test will enable you to judge your increasing speed, accuracy and endurance!

2 Practise the speed tests on the following pages by sorting out the difficult words, typing these until you feel confident and can type them at some speed. Next, decide if any difficulty has been experienced with the typing of certain phrases. After practising these to build up speed, you are then ready to try the speed test itself.

3 Never erase any mistakes as this is a waste of time.

4 Set the timer for the time span you decide upon, say three minutes to begin with, then commence typing immediately you have set the timer.

5 Stop typing when you hear the buzzer.

6 Calculate your speed as follows, using the counted tests on the following pages: Add the total number of *strokes achieved* (you will find a running total at the end of each line) and *divide this total by five* to obtain the number of words typed in three minutes. Then *divide the total number of words by three* and you will see how fast you can type in words per minute (wpm).

*Example:* 600 *strokes typed in three mns*

600 *divided by five to obtain number of words*

= *120 words typed in three mns*

= 120 *divided by three* = 40 wpm

7 Calculate whether your number of errors is within an acceptable limit (see below) and you will find that your achievements are well worth all the effort expended.

## Calculation of errors

**Option 1:** maximum allowance of one error for every 50 words typed (so in the above example, allow two errors for the 120 words).

**Option 2:** six-error allowance is made for a five minute speed test (speed is calculated on words typed up to the seventh error)

**Option 3:** one-error allowed for percentage of words, i.e. two or three per 100.

Types of error include: faulty spacing after punctuation marks; transposed words or letters; words omitted or inserted; lines omitted; paragraphs haphazardly indented (indents are rarely used now); misspellings, etc.

Remember that, when attempting the tests, speed without accuracy is valueless. It is far better to have good quality than indifferent quantity, and an excellent motto to keep continually in mind is to 'make haste slowly'.

## Exercise 54

Do not type the numbers in the right-hand column

| | |
|---|---|
| If you are using a word processor to write articles, business | 62 |
| letters or memoranda, it is very useful to explore or to consider | 128 |
| what possibilities there are available to you within the software. | 195 |
| Some authors need the facility of a prepared layout with margins, | 262 |
| tabs, formatting, etc and when this is provided it is called a | 325 |
| template. It is especially useful for long reports or extended | 390 |
| documents to be printed on A4 paper or continuous stationery. | 452 |
| For this type of work a special set of templates is provided | 513 |
| from which a choice can be made. Each template has different | 575 |
| settings to suit individual needs. Usually the pages are numbered | 642 |
| at the bottom with a page number provided on the right-hand margin | 709 |
| at the end of each page. This is particularly useful for | 766 |
| documents and numbered pages of reports. | 806 |

(161 words)

## Exercise 55

```
Portable language translators are an innovation which enables the    65
user to carry and use the equivalent of a large number of           123
dictionaries. They operate with a visible word display and all      187
that the user needs to do is to key in which language he wishes      251
his word or phrase to be translated into. Up to six European        312
languages can be combined in one translator which is small enough   378
to be carried in a pocket or handbag. However, no help is given     443
with an audio input so that the person using the translator does    509
not know how to pronounce the words. A language laboratory,         570
however, provides input of both written and aural information thus  637
giving the fullest experience of the new skill. It is considered    703
to be one of the most effective ways of learning a foreign          762
language with a correct pronunciation.                              800
```

(160 words)

## Exercise 56

The World Wide Web is the most colourful and, for many people,          63
the most useful aspect of the Internet. It consists of billions         127
of pages of information, stored on computers throughout the             187
world. The pages contain text, graphics, video clips, sounds and        252
most importantly - hyperlinks to other pages. A text item or            315
image on a Web page can hold a hyperlink joining it to another          378
page, which may be in the same computer, or in another machine          441
the other side of the World. Hyperlinks can also be used to             501
connect to files and to e-mail addresses. To access the World           563
Wide Web, you need a web browser. This is a program which can           625
display the text and images that make up Web pages and which can        690
interpret the links that take you from one page to another.             750
Working with other software, browsers can also handle all kinds         814
of graphics, audio/video clips, multimedia displays and other           876
types of files that can be found on the Web.                            920

(184 words)

## Exercise 57

It is now easy to arrange and to prepare standard letters       58
on word processors and store the texts on disc. A list of       116
names and addresses can be also stored in the computer's        173
files. Then a technique known as 'mail merge' is used to        232
prepare data to circularise a particular letter to the names    293
and addresses listed. The computer can personalise each         350
addressee's details, eg Miss S Johnson, 6 Hill Street,          405
Sleaford. It also amends the salutation in each instance        463
to correspond, ie 'Dear Miss Johnson'. It can also              516
change the contents of the letter to correspond with the        573
individual's details using phrases like 'the Johnson            628
family has been chosen to receive' included in the body of      797
the letter. In this way the recipient feels that he or          743
she is receiving a letter meant for him or her alone.           797
The names and addresses can be transferred from any list        854
of mailing addresses to other files for the corresponding       912
address labels to be swiftly produced. Word processors          968
are also suitable for printing data on envelopes.               1018

(203 words)

## Exercise 58

| | |
|---|---:|
| Electronic mail is the simplest and the most widely used of all | 63 |
| the Internet's facilities. It is mainly used for sending plain | 126 |
| text, but you can attach graphics, documents and other files to | 190 |
| messages. E-mail speeds up communications. Even a long text | 250 |
| message takes only a few seconds to send and will normally reach | 315 |
| its destination within a few minutes. Of course, when messages | 378 |
| get read is another matter. Some people only pick up their mail | 442 |
| once a day, and may not read all of the messages when they | 501 |
| arrive. E-mail can be written and read while you are online, but | 566 |
| is best managed offline. This way, the telephone line is only in | 630 |
| use for as long as it takes to transmit pre-written messages and | 695 |
| to download incoming mail. It doesn't just reduce your costs, it | 760 |
| also avoids the possibility of losing a connection half-way | 820 |
| through writing a message, and it gives you time to check your | 883 |
| text for typing and spelling errors first. When sending | 939 |
| messages, you must get the e-mail addresses exactly right, or | 1001 |
| the post won't get through. | 1029 |

(205 words)

14 speed tests

## Exercise 59

Among the many other facilities provided by computers is          57
the ability to prepare business forms, invoices, statements,      117
orders, etc. Computers can also make calculations of gross        176
total prices, value-added tax, discounts, and net prices.         233
The many computerised procedures available today include          289
telephone directories, electronic mail, networks and file         346
sharing. It has also recently been made possible to give 24-      406
hour warnings of impending floods and other disasters by the      466
information calculated on computers owned by some insurance       525
companies; and these companies are now able to supply their       585
clients with notification in time for evasive action to be        643
taken. Doctors and surgeons increasingly use computers            698
for the storage and retrieval of information about patients,      758
about various symptoms of illnesses and the many different        816
methods of treatment available.                                   849

(170 *words*)

**Exercise 60**

An alternative to speaker presentations, as such, is
called "interactive multi-media". A computer is used to
store a variety of presentation material such as text,
pictures, sound and video clips. The person using the
computer presses a touch screen or cursor to activate
a specific part of the picture. This triggers an event,
eg the display, more text or the playing of a video clip.
The experience for the user is almost like playing a
video game but the intention is to educate and inform.
A recent example of multi-media is the "Virtual
Museum". This is a computerised library of visual
information so accessible that it allows the person using
it to walk round (to the sound of footsteps) in an
imaginary science or art museum. Upon 'entering' the
foyer he or she can click onto a particular choice of
subject material on display - choices include animation,
picture, static display of a work of art, treasure,
scientific marvel or discovery (recently updated) etc.

53
109
164
218
272
328
386
439
494
544
595
653
705
759
813
870
921
976

1027
1085
1141
1196
1251
1308
1363
1420
1471

The person can then again walk through the various
doorways and into the museum rooms. Having decided, one
goes through the doorway, enters the chosen 'room' and
views the moving computer graphic data, eg a video or
animated clip about each topic, rotating each wall in
turn to include the whole room. The main advantages of
these interactive multi-media are that the person using
the presentations can learn about what interests him or
her at a chosen pace and from a vast choice of subjects.

(294 words)

# 15 difficult spellings

Correct spelling, like punctuation, is essential to the production of good typewritten work. You should always run the spell checker after you have finished typing a document – even the best spellers make typing errors. The checker should pick up any mistakes and give you a chance to correct them, but you will save yourself time if you get more of your spellings right first time.

A selected list of difficult spellings is given below, and includes common words which often cause problems – such as *accommodate, gauge* and *seize* – as well as words which are in general business use. It is recommended that each page of the list should be typed, in order to impress the correct spelling on the mind. The meaning of the words is equally important, and a dictionary should be consulted where there is any doubt.

| | | |
|---|---|---|
| abhor | aerial | apparently |
| abhorred | affect | appealing |
| abolish | aggregate | appendix |
| abscess | aggrieved | appropriate |
| accede | aghast | argument |
| accept | agreeable | ascend |
| access | allege | asset |
| accessible | allegiance | assuage |
| accommodation | alliance | asterisk |
| accumulate | allotment | atrocious |
| achieve | aluminium | auspicious |
| achieving | amateur | authentic |
| aching | ambiguity | authenticity |
| acknowledge | ameliorate | auxiliary |
| acquiesce | amicable | |
| acquire | ampersand | bankruptcy |
| adherence | analogous | banquet |
| adjournment | analyse | basically |
| admissible | analysis | bazaar |
| adolescent | anomalous | belief |
| advantageous | appal | believable |
| advertise | appalling | believe |
| advertisement | apparent | beneficiaries |

beneficiary
benefit
benefited
bilateral
biography
bona fide
book-keeping
boycott
brilliance
brittle
budget
budgeting
buoy
bureaucracy
bureaucrat
by-election
by-law
by-product

cafeteria
calamitous
camouflage
canister
career
carousel
casualty
catalogue
catarrh
catastrophe
ceiling
changeable
chaos
chaotic
chargeable
chauffeur
chronological
coefficient
coincide

coinciding
collateral
colleague
colloquial
collusion
combustible
commitment
committal
compatibility
compatible
comprehensible
comprehensive
computerisation
compulsory
conceivable
conglomerate
connoisseur
conscientious
conspicuous
consummate
contentious
continent
controversy
conversation
conversion
corduroy
corollary
corroborate
corruptible
counterfeit
credible
crucial
cul-de-sac
curriculum

debacle
debar
debarred

debutante
decree
decreeing
defensible
defer
deferred
deficiency
deficient
demarcation
dependant (of)
dependent (on)
deprecate
depreciate
descendant
destructible
deterioration
deter
deterrent
develop
development
dial
dialling
diaphragm
dilemma
disc
discern
discernible
discreet
discretion
discretionary
disk
dissatisfaction
disseminate
disservice
dissuade
doubtful
dubitable
dynamic

earnest
eavesdrop
ecclesiastical
ecstasy
edible
efficient
eligible
elucidate
embarrass
enamel
enamelled
encumbrance
encyclopaedia
entrepreneur
epitome
equanimity
equitable
equivalent
erstwhile
et cetera
etiquette
evaporate
exacerbate
exchange
exchangeable
excusable
excuse
exorbitant
extraneous
extra-curricular
extraditable
exuberant
eyewitness

facetious
facial
facile
fallacious

fatigue
feasible
February
fiasco
fibreglass
fictitious
flammable
flotation
focus
formally
formerly
   (previously)
fortuitous
freeing
fulfil
fulfilled
fulfilment

gauge
gauging
gazetteer
glossary
gratuitous
guarantor
gullible
gymnasium

haphazard
harass
hazardous
heterogeneous
honourable
honorary
humorist
humour
hydrangea
hygiene
hypothesis

idiosyncrasy
ignominious
illiteracy
illiterate
illusion
imminent
immovable
impracticable
impromptu
incognito
incur
incurred
independence
indict
indictment
infinitesimal
inflammable
ingenious
ingenuous
install
instalment
interim
irreducible
irresistible
itinerary

janitor
jargon
jeopardise
jewellery
judiciary
judicious
juxtaposition
kilogram
kilometre
kilowatt
kudos

label
labelled
laborious
liaison
libel
libellous
litigation

maestro
magnanimous
magnate
magnetise
maintenance
maisonette
malingerer
malleable
malpractice
manage
manageable
manoeuvre
marshalled
massacre
miniature
misapprehend
mis-statement
monetary
mortgage
mystery

naive
necessary
necessitate
nomenclature
nondescript
nonplussed
notable
notice
noticeable

nowadays
nullify

obituary
obsession
occur
occurrence
omission
omit
omitted
onerous
ophthalmic
ostentatious
outrageous
overrate
oxy-acetylene

panel
panelled
paraffin
parallel
paralleled
parcel
parcelled
pastime
pecuniary
penultimate
perceivable
perceive
perceptible
peremptory
permissible
permit
persecute
personal
personnel
persuade
persuasive

pessimism
phantom
phenomenal
phenomenon
pharmaceutical
pharmacology
pharyngitis
phenobarbitone
phlox
phobia
phonetic
phosphorus
plagiarise
pneumatic
postcard
posthumous
practice (noun)
practise (verb)
precede
predecessor
prefer
preferred
principal (chief)
principle
proceed
process
proffer
programme *(but
computer program)*
pronounce
pronounceable
pronunciation
propitious
pseudonym
psychology
purchasable
pursue
putrefy

quandary
quantitative
quarrel
quarrelled
queue

rateable
readdress
rearrange
receivable
reciprocate
recur
recurrence
removable
rendezvous
reprehensible
rescind
rescission
résumé
reversible
rhythm
rival
rivalled
rudimentary

sceptic
scepticism
scrutineer
secession
secretary
secretariat
segregate
seizable
seize
separate

silhouette
simultaneously
skiing
skilful
sophisticated
sovereignty
spontaneous
stationary (not
   moving)
stationery
   (envelopes, etc)
statistician
stencilled
stereotyped
subsidiary
succeed
succession
succinct
sue
suggest
suggestible
suing
supercilious
supersede
surreptitious
susceptibility
susceptible
suspension
synonymous
synthesis

tautology
teetotaller
temporary
tinge

tingeing
trademark
transfer
transferable
transferred
triumph
tunnel
tunnelled

ubiquitous
unanimous
unilateral
unkempt
unnecessary
unparalleled
utilitarian

vapour
vaporise
vehicular
veil
vigorous
vigour
voracious

wilful
witticism
word processors

yardstick

zany
zapped
Zephyr
zoology

# 16

## abbreviations

Abbreviations are shortened forms of words and phrases, consisting in many cases only of initials, which have become established by common usage. The following list is not exhaustive, but it does include most of the abbreviations in general business use.

The use of the full stop will depend on whether open or closed punctuation is employed. Note, however, that certain signs and symbols should never take a full stop, for example the £ or $ sign, the ampersand (&) and @ (at). In addition, full stops should not be used after abbreviations of units of measurement, such as ft, mm and kg.

**&** and (ampersand)
**@** at, for
**£** pound sterling
**$** dollar (money)
**%** per cent
**%0** per thousand

**A1** first class, first rate
**a. a. r.** against all risks
**ab init** *ab initio* (Latin), from the beginning
**abt** about
**a/c, acct** account A/C account
**ack** acknowledge
**AD** *Anno Domini* (Latin), in the year of our Lord
**ad, advt** advertisement
**ad lib** *ad libitum* (Latin), at pleasure
**ad val** *ad valorem* (Latin), according to value
**AGM** Annual General Meeting
**agt** agreement; agent
**accom** accommodation
**a.m.** *ante meridiem* (Latin), before noon
**amt** amount

**anon** anonymous
**ans** answer
**A/P** accounts payable
**appro** approval, approbation
**approx** approximate
**appt(s)** appointments
**A/R** accounts receivable
**A/S** account sales
**a.s.a.p.** as soon as possible
**asst** assistant
**av, ave** average

**BA** Bachelor of Arts
**bal** balance
**b/d** bring (brought) down
**B/D** Bank Draft
**B/E** bill of exchange
**bel** believe
**b/f** bring (brought) forward
**bk** book
**B/L** bill of lading
**B/P** bill payable
**B/R** bill receivable
**Bro, Bros** brother, brothers
**B/S** balance sheet; bill of sale
**BSc** Bachelor of Science
**bus** business

c cent(s)
C centigrade, celsius
C/A Capital Account
carr. pd carriage paid
carr. fwd carriage forward
cat catalogue
cc cubic centimetre; carbon copy
c/d carried down
cf. compare
c/f carried forward
C & F cost and freight
ch, chap chapter
chq cheque
c.i.f. cost, insurance and freight
cm centimetre
C/N credit note
Co Company
c/o care of; carried over
COD cash on delivery
col. column
comm Commission
cont continued
cr credit, creditor
cres crescent
CS Civil Service
ctte committee
cum div with the dividend
c.w.o. cash with order

D/A Deposit Account
DB Day Book
D/D Demand Draft
Deb. Debenture
def definitely
dely, d/y delivery
dept department
dev develop

dft draft
disc discount
div dividends; division
D/N Debit Note
do. ditto (the same)
doz dozen
D/P documents against payment
dr debtor, debit
Dr Doctor or Dear
d/s days after sight
D.v. *Deo volente* (Latin), God willing

ea each
ed edition, editor
e.g. for example (*exampli gratia*)
enc enclosure(s)
E&OE errors and omissions excepted
esp especially
Esq Esquire
est established; estimated
et al *et alia* (Latin), and others
ETA estimated time of arrival
etc *et cetera* (Latin), and the rest
ETD estimated time of departure
et seq *et sequentia* (Latin), and the following
ex without or exercise
exch. exchange
ex div without dividends
ex int not including interest
exors executors
exp express or experience
exs expenses

**f, fr** franc(s)
**F, Fahr** Fahrenheit
**f.a.a.** free of all average (used in marine insurance)
**FAO** for the attention of
**f.a.q.** free alongside quay; fair average quality
**FAQ** Frequently Asked Questions
**f.a.s.** free alongside ship
**Feb** February
**fcp, fcap** foolscap
**f.d.** free docks
**ffly** faithfully
**f.i.f.o.** first in, first out
**fig(s)** figure(s)
**f.i.t.** free of income tax
**fo, fol** folio
**FO** Firm Order
**f.o.b.** free on board
**f.o.r.** free on rail
**fp** fully paid
**fr** from
**Fri** Friday
**frt** freight
**ft** foot, feet
**fwd** forward
**fyi** for your information

**g** gramme
**GA** general average (insurance)
**gen** general
**GM** General Manager
**GMT** Greenwich Mean Time
**gntee(s)** guarantee(s)
**Gov** Governor
**Govt** Government
**gr** grain, grammar

**gr. wt.** gross weight
**HMSO** Her Majesty's Stationery Office
**HO** Head Office
**Hon.** Honorary, Honourable
**h.p.** horse power
**HP** hire purchase
**HQ** headquarters
**hr(s)** hour(s)

**ib, ibid** *ibidem* (Latin), in the same place
**IB** Invoice Book
**IBI** Invoice Book Inwards
**i/c** in charge
**i.e.** *id est* (Latin), that is
**I/F** insufficient funds (banking)
**immed** immediate
**IMF** International Monetary Fund
**inc** incorporated
**ins** insurance
**inst** instant, current month
**int** interest
**inv** invoice
**IOU** I owe you
**ital** italics
**IQ** Intelligence Quotient

**J/A** Joint Account
**Jan** January
**JP** Justice of the Peace
**Jun, Jr** Junior

**kg, kilo** kilogramme
**kl** kilolitre(s)
**km** kilometre(s)
**kw** kilowatts

l, lt litre(s)
lat latitude
lb pound (weight)
l.c. lower case
L/C Letter of Credit
Led Ledger
LGA Local Government
 Authority
l.i.f.o. last in, first out
long longitude
Ltd limited

m metre (s), minutes, million
max maximum
MC Master of Ceremonies
M/d months after date
med medium
mem, memo memorandum
Messrs *Messieurs* (French),
 Gentlemen
mfg manufacturing
mfr manufacturer
mg milligram
mgr manager
min minimum, minute
MIP Marine Insurance Policy
misc miscellaneous
ml millilitre(s)
mm millimetre(s)
Mme Madame
MO Medical Officer; money
 order
Mon Monday
MP Member of Parliament;
 Military Police
m.p.h. miles per hour
m/s months after sight; metre
 per second

ms(s) manuscript(s)
MSc Master of Science

n.a. not available
N/A no advice; not acceptable
 (banking); not applicable
NB *nota bene* (Latin), mark
 well, note well
necy necessary
nem con *nemme contradicente*
 (Latin), no one against
N/F no funds (banking)
nil *nihil* (Latin), nothing
N/m no mark
N/O no orders (trading) nom.
 nominal
NP Notary Public
nr near

o/a on account of
o/c over charge; officer com-
 manding; out of charge
o/d on demand
O/D overdraft, overdrawn
OK all correct
O&M Organisation and
 Methods
o/p out of print
op cit *opere citato* (Latin), in
 the work cited
opp. opposed, opposite or
 opportunities
OR owner's risk
ord. ordinary
o/s out of stock; outstanding

p, pp page, pages
p.a. *per annum* (Latin), yearly

**PAYE** pay as you earn (taxation)

**p.c.** per cent

**PC** personal computer, police constable

**P/c** price current

**p.c.b.** petty cash book

**pcl** parcel

**pcs** pieces

**pd** paid

**per** by

**per capita** by the head

**per prop**, **pp** *per procurationem* (Latin), on behalf of

**pkg** package

**P & L** Profit and Loss

**PLC** Public Limited Company

**p.m.** *post meridiem* (Latin), afternoon

**p.n** promissory note

**P.O.** postal order; post office

**pp** parcel post

**p. & p.** postage and packing

**pr** pair, price

**pref** preference, preferred

**prepd** prepared

**prima facie** at first sight

**Prof** Professor

**pro forma** as a matter of form

**pro tem** *pro tempore* (Latin), for the time being

**PS** postscript

**PTO** please turn over

**PV** per value, present value

**qu** query, question

**quan**, **qty** quantity

**qr** quarter

**R/D** refer to drawer (banking)

**re** with reference to, concerning

**rec** receive

**rec(t)** receipt

**recd** received

**recom** recommend

**ref** reference

**refd** referred

**reg**, **regd** registered

**rep** report; representative

**req** required

**resp** responsible

**retd** returned

**rd** road

**rly** railway

**rm** ream

**R/p** reply paid

**RSVP** *Répondez, s'il vous plaît* (French), please reply

**Sat** Saturday

**SB** sales book

**sch** school; schedule

**sec** second or secretary

**sep** separate

**sgn** sign(ed)

**sh** shall

**shd** should

**sig(s)** signature

**S/N** shipping note

**soc** society

**spec** specification, speculation

**sq** square

**SS** steamship

**St.** Saint; street; station

**std** standard

**stet** let it stand

**stg** sterling (money)

stk stock
suff sufficient
Sun Sunday

temp temporary
thro through
Thurs Thursday
TMO telegraph money order
TO, t/o turnover
Tr Trustee
TT telegraphic transfer
Tue Tuesday

u.c. upper case
ult. *ultimo* (Latin), last month;
    ultimatum
u/w underwriter

v., vs versus (Latin); against
var variety
VAT Value Added Tax
VHF very high frequency
via by way of, through

viz *videlicet* (Latin), namely
vol volume

w with
W/B Waybill
wd would
Wed Wednesday
w.e.f. with effect from
wh which
whf wharf
wi will
wk(s) week; weeks
w.p.m. words per minute
wt, wgt weight

x.d. ex dividend (without
    dividend)
x.int. ex interest (without
    interest)

yr(s) year(s)
yrs yours

# 17

# key to the
# exercises

HOME ADDRESS

Today's Date

Westoby & Sheerwater PLC
369 Church St Gardens
EDMONTON
N9 7 YT

Dear Sirs

POST AS PERSONAL ADMINISTRATOR - PERSONNEL
DEPT

I am enclosing my application form for the above post in your
Company.

Should I be fortunate enough to be considered as a possible
candidate I would be able to attend an interview at any time to suit
you except on Monday, 14 July, when I have to attend a
Conference in Glasgow on behalf of my Company.

Yours faithfully


A L Jones (Mr)

enc

# Key to exercise 41

**WESTOBY & SHEERWATER PLC**
369 Church Street Gardens
EDMONTON N9 7YT

**JOB APPLICATION FORM**

Title of Job ...................................................... Dept ..................................

APPLICANT'S FULL NAME (BLOCK CAPITALS)

SURNAME .................................... FIRST NAMES ..................................

ADDRESS ................................................................................................

.............................................................. POST CODE ..........................

DATE OF BIRTH .............................. NATIONALITY ...........................

EDUCATIONAL QUALIFICATIONS (Please give dates)

**School.** .................................................................................................

..............................................................................................................

**College** .................................................................................................

**Other** ...................................................................................................

**Typing Speed** (if applicable) .............................................. wpm

EXPERIENCE (Please give dates)

| Job Title | Company Name | Dates |
|-----------|--------------|-------|
| ........................................ | ........................................ | ..................... |
| ........................................ | ........................................ | ..................... |
| ........................................ | ........................................ | ..................... |

**Salary Required** ............................................... pa

REASONS FOR APPLYING FOR THIS POST

..............................................................................................................

..............................................................................................................

Signed. ............................................................. Date. ...................................

## *Jonathan Henry Miller* & *Sons PLC*

ESTATE AGENTS
9 WEST FRONT
CAMBRIDGE
CB1 8DR
*Tel* 01223 686 00777          *Fax* 01223 866 44335

Our ref DM/JR/BEECH

19 March 200-

Mr F R Finlay
Drover's Cottage
High Street
HORRINGER
IP32 1QR

Dear Mr Finlay

RE PURCHASE OF FLAT AT 15 BEECH MEWS E9 3XL

I am writing to confirm that I have put forward your offer of
£195,500 to Miss Baine, the Vendor. She has accepted this offer
with the proviso that, as the figure is lower than the asking price of
£205,000, she is not prepared to include the carpets, curtains and
light fittings in the sale.

Please let me know as soon as possible what your views are.

Yours sincerely


DOROTHY MILLER
Manager

### *Jonathan Henry Miller & Sons PLC*

ESTATE AGENTS
9 WEST FRONT
CAMBRIDGE
CB1 8DR
*Tel* 01223 686 00777          *Fax* 01223 866 44335

Our ref SJ/BC

3 June 200-

Dr Frederic Avey
10 Birch Avenue
Church Street
EDMONTON N9 9XV

Dear Dr Avey

SALE OF THE THATCHED COTTAGE, LYLE LANE,
GODMASTON, CAMBRIDGE CB19 lBR

We are pleased to advise you that we have placed an advertisement
in a local paper with a large distribution area offering your
property for sale at the agreed price of £150,000. The paper will be
published on Friday of this week and we anticipate a good response
to our advertising.

If we receive any offers for your property, we shall immediately
contact you and take instructions regarding the sale. It is always
advisable to be prepared to accept an offer if this falls within your
financial expectation, and we have priced your property at a
suitable figure to enable you to do this.

If we can be of any further assistance, please do not hesitate to
contact us. In the meantime we will continue to show prospective
purchasers round your property.

Yours sincerely
Sandra Johnson
Property Consultant

# Key to exercise 45

MEMORANDUM

TO Sandra Johnson, Property Consultant

FROM Natalie Miller, Executive Director

DATE 4 April 200-

ADVERTISEMENTS FOR NEW PROPERTIES

I am sending you the 3 latest advertisements which we need to publish in the "Huntingdon and Cambridge Weekly Herald" this week.

Please check that all the details are correct - price, description, etc and then notify the clients that we are advertising their properties for sale as from next Friday's edition.

The photographs are arriving from the processors tomorrow. I think you will find that the "Herald" needs to have our advertisements 4 days before publication. This is a new expanding local paper with a distribution which covers a wide area around Cambridge and Huntingdon and we should have some good response to our advertisement.

I would appreciate any comments on potential improvements etc which you may wish to make as I sometimes feel that our descriptions of properties could be more dynamic and appealing.

1) Deceptively spacious thatched cottage with good sized grounds, situated in quiet village opposite church - 3 beds, 2 rec, garage, stable block and barn. £150,000. Ref QD 46. (GODMASTON)

2) Beautifully refurbished detached house in semi-rural position with large gardens, garage, 3 beds, large kitchen. £232,000. Ref QD 47. (CLAYTONBURY)

3) Just reduced for quick sale - 4 bed terraced Georgian house in city centre, 3 reception rooms, off-street parking for 3 cars, short distance from river (mooring rights also available) £260,000. Ref QD 48. (CAMBRIDGE)

Please let me know as soon as you have organised this and send me a copy of the PROOFS.

# Key to exercise 46

## THE PROPERTY LETTING CENTRE

Head Office    24 Lynton Close    Elm End Road
WATFORD    WD3 7KM

Telephone 01923 1200099                    FAX 01923 1226565

Our ref: BKC/WM/ht

4 September 200-

Mr D A V Jackson
Avenida de Alvarode
Vascenceles 2993
2711 SINTRA
Portugal

Dear Mr Jackson

Re: 15 Beechwood Mews, Harewood St., Potters Bar

Further to our visit to the above flat on 31 August 200-, we are pleased to confirm that, as agreed, we have placed details of the property on our books at a rental charge of £520 per calendar month.

As you are aware, the rental income will be inclusive of maintenance, ground rent, and water rate for which you are currently responsible. The services such as Gas, Telephone and Electricity will be payable by the Tenants who will be informed by us to sign for the source of supply prior to occupation.

We always advertise our properties only to professional persons and we take up their references on your behalf. A deposit of one month's rental plus £100 booking fee is paid to us plus the one month's rental in advance. We then deduct our fees from this sum and forward to you an account plus the balance of the monies due to you. If you require any alteration to this arrangement, ie for this Company to pay the monies into an English bank account on your behalf we shall be pleased to do this for you.

2
4 September 200-
Mr D A V Jackson

It may be that you will find you will need to make use of our full property management service whilst you are staying for an indefinite period abroad, and, if you require any further information, please do not hesitate to contact us. In the meantime I enclose our brochure containing details of the full management service we provide.

Yours sincerely

WENDY MACPHERSON
Property Letting Manager

enc

## Key to exercise 47

# THE PROPERTY LETTING CENTRE

THIS BROCHURE is to give you information regarding our two services of property letting. Both services include a free valuation of your property by our expert valuer to ascertain that a correct rental is to be charged.

The first, which is a full management service, guarantees that this Company will find you a suitable professional person to rent your property for six-monthly (or one-yearly) periods. The Company takes up full financial and personal references on your behalf and collects the rents as and when these become due. A full Tenancy Agreement is drawn up and signed by both parties. The full management service means that you have peace of mind as, should any repairs etc become necessary, the Company arranges for the appropriate work to be carried out, and debits your account accordingly. This is a particularly suitable service for owners who are too busy to supervise the lettings personally or who are living abroad. There is a charge of 12 per cent for this service.

We offer the second service which is a PART MANAGEMENT SERVICE where this Company guarantees to find a suitable professional person to rent your property for six-monthly or one-yearly periods. The Company takes up full financial and personal references on your behalf and collects the rents as and when due. A Full Tenancy Agreement is drawn up and signed by both parties. This is a suitable service for owners who are able to personally supervise the letting and arrange their own repairs. There is a charge of 10 per cent for this service. Should you require to change over from the part management service to full management at any time during the tenancy period this can be arranged at a fee of two per cent extra.

In both services the Tenant will be asked to provide a deposit of ONE MONTH'S RENTAL in advance and to pay his or her rent by standing order at a bank or through a building society.

35 East Barnes Avenue
Dykes Burn
MIDDLESBROUGH
Cleveland
NT3 3LK
Telephone No 0642 87 224439

24 September 200-

The Manager
Property Letting Centre
24 Lynton Close
Elm End Road
WATFORD WD3 7KM

Dear Sir

With reference to your advertisement in today's edition of the
'Daily Provincial and Cleveland Echo', I shall be grateful if you will
kindly send me as soon as possible details of the two flats you have
available - reference numbers G789 and G901.

I am commencing work in Central London on 10 October and am
urgently in need of a fully furnished two bedroom flat near to a
railway station that would be convenient for commuting to
Liverpool Street station. The maximum rental I am prepared to pay
is £180 per week or £750 per calendar month.

The flat must have an automatic washing machine, tumble dryer,
fridge, freezer, cooker extractor hood, and some form of central
heating. I do also need good parking facilities to be available
nearby, preferably on the premises.

In order to save time I am enclosing the names and addresses of
two referees to whom you can write and you will note that one is
my employer in Middlesbrough for whom I have worked for five
years.

2
24 September 200-
Property Letting Centre

I plan to visit London on 28 September and, if I like the flat after viewing it, I shall be prepared to sign a contract immediately and move in on 30 September or as soon after that date as is possible.

Thank you for your help in this matter.

Yours faithfully


Belinda Richardson (Miss)
enc

## Key to exercise 49

```
LIST OF SUBJECTS

Accountancy      Dietetics        Mathematics      Printing
Advertising      Economics        Metallurgy       Refrigeration
Aeronautics      Elocution        Mineralogy       Salesmanship
Architecture     Engineering      Mining           Shipping
Arithmetic       English          Music            Shorthand
Banking          First-Aid        Needlework       Sociology
Book-keeping     Geography        Optics           Telecommunications
Building         History          Pharmacy         Television
Calculations     Insurance        Photography      Theatre
Chemistry        Investment       Physics          Transport
Commerce         Journalism       Poetry           Typewriting
```

# Key to exercise 52

ELECTRA MACHINE

<u>Quarterly Sales</u>

| <u>Branch</u> | <u>March</u> | <u>June</u> | <u>Sept</u> | <u>Dec</u> |
|---|---|---|---|---|
| Southampton | 136 | 210 | 195 | 187 |
| Portsmouth | 125 | 167 | 154 | 170 |
| Liverpool | 103 | 141 | 139 | 126 |
| Birmingham | 214 | 230 | 179 | 223 |
| Manchester | 212 | 176 | 194 | 182 |
| Leeds | 317 | 265 | 276 | 284 |
| Sheffield | 284 | 314 | 237 | 330 |
| Burnley | 147 | 201 | 169 | 229 |
| Middlesbrough | 231 | 198 | 217 | 186 |
| Cardiff | 246 | 312 | 256 | 306 |
| Swansea | 193 | 224 | 184 | 219 |
| Newport | <u>231</u> | <u>189</u> | <u>209</u> | <u>196</u> |
| Totals | <u>2,439</u> | <u>2,627</u> | <u>2,409</u> | <u>2,638</u> |

**taking it further**

If you have been learning touch typing to improve your career prospects, you should now think about getting your new skills recognised with a qualification. City & Guilds have a number of schemes covering different aspects of typing and keyboarding. Find out more at their Web site: **www.city-and-guilds.co.uk**. The OCR examinations group also offer keyboarding skills certificates. For more on those, visit the OCR site at **www.ocr.org.uk**.

There is far more to learn about word processing than has been covered in this book – we have only scratched the surface of what is possible. Microsoft Word allows you to control almost every aspect of the appearance and layout of text, and has facilities, such as 'mail merge' (used for creating personalised letters) which can simplify and speed up office work. Try *Teach Yourself Word* if you would like to learn more about Word.

You may also want to think about acquiring a wider range of computer skills, and about getting recognition for those skills. OCR's CLAIT (Computer Literacy and Information Technology) award is widely accepted as showing a good level of competence in key aspects of information technology. You can read more about this at the OCR site at **www.ocr.org.uk**, and *Teach Yourself CLAIT* gives a full coverage of the syllabus.

# index

Abbreviations  180–185
Agenda  127
Alignment  92
Ampersand  83
Apostrophe  78
ASCII numbers  60
At sign @  83
Attention line  105

Backup files  108
Bold  89
Borders  154
Business letters  103

Capitals  83
Caps Lock  50
Clipboard  8
Closed punctuation  85
Colon  80
Comma  79
Complimentary close  107
Confidential  105
Continuation sheets  106
Copies  108
Copying practice  63
Correction signs  132
Courtesy titles  111
Cut, Copy and Paste  8

Dash  79
Date, in letters  104
Documents and files, in Word  12

Ellipsis  81
Em dash  79
Emphasis  89
En dash  79
Enclosures  108
Envelopes  111
Errors  6
    calculation of  163

Figures and symbols  43
Files, open and close  13
Font size  89
Fonts  88
Formatting text  88
Full stop  80

Guide keys  21
Gutter  9

Handwritten copy  132
Hanging indent  91
Home keys  21
Hyphenation  82, 92

Indents  91
Insert/Overwrite text modes  6
Insets  106
Inside name and address  105
Italics  89

Justification  92

Keyboard practice  22
Keyboard, standard  17

Landscape orientation  10
Layout  108
Leader characters  151
Letter headings  104
Line spacing  94
Lines and borders  154

Margins  9, 103
Meetings  127
Memorandums  114
Minutes  129
Mirror margins  9

Open punctuation  84
Orientation  10

Paper size  10, 103
Paragraph formatting  91
Paragraphs, spacing  95
Parentheses  82
Per cent sign %  83
Personal  105
Points  89
Portrait orientation  10
Postcards  115
Printing  14
Private  105
Punctuation and spacing  63
Punctuation marks  78

Question mark  82
Quotation marks  83
Qwerty keyboard  2, 17

Reference initials  104
Repetition practice  162
Roman numerals  58
Ruler  91

Salutation  105
Sans serif fonts  89
Saving documents  12
Semicolon  80
Serif fonts  88
Shift keys  50
Signatures  107
Special characters  59
Spell checking  100
Strokes and words  162
Subject heading  105
Symbol dialog box  59
Symbols, in Word  59

Tables  153
Tabs  150
Templates  97
Text
    editing  7
    entering  6
    formatting  88
    selecting  7
Touch method  17

Underline  89

Word  4
Word processors  3
WordPad  3
Wordwrap  6
Work station  3